Why It's OK
to Be a Sports
Fan

This book offers readers a pitch-side view of the ethics of fandom. Its accessible six chapters are aimed both at true sports fans whose conscience may be occasionally piqued by their pastime, and at those who are more certain of the moral hazards involved in following a team or sport.

Why It's OK to Be a Sports Fan wrestles with a range of arguments against fandom and counters with its own arguments on why being a fan is very often a good thing. It looks at the ethical issues that fans face, from the violent or racist behavior of those in the stands, to players' infamous misdeeds, to owners debasing their own clubs. In response to these moral risks, the book argues that by being *critical fans*, followers of a team or individual can reap the benefits of fandom while avoiding many of the ethical pitfalls. The authors show the value in deeply loving a team but also how a condition of this value is recognizing that the love of a fan comes with real limits and responsibilities.

Alfred Archer is Associate Professor of Philosophy at Tilburg University in the Netherlands. He is the author (with Benjamin Matheson) of *Honouring and Admiring the Immoral: An Ethical Guide* (2021) and the co-editor of *Emotions in Sport and Games* (2021), *Self-Sacrifice and Moral Philosophy* (2020), and *The Moral Psychology of Admiration* (2019).

Jake Wojtowicz received his PhD on ethics and the philosophy of law from King's College London in 2019. He lives with his wife Hannah and their pets, Archie and Genny, in Rochester, NY and is adjusting to life as a Buffalo Bills fan.

Why It's OK: The Ethics and Aesthetics of How We Live

ABOUT THE SERIES:

Philosophers often build cogent arguments for unpopular positions. Recent examples include cases against marriage and pregnancy, for treating animals as our equals, and dismissing some popular art as aesthetically inferior. What philosophers have done less often is to offer compelling arguments for widespread and established human behavior, like getting married, having children, eating animals, and going to the movies. But if one role for philosophy is to help us reflect on our lives and build sound justifications for our beliefs and actions, it seems odd that philosophers would neglect arguments for the lifestyles most people—including many philosophers—actually lead. Unfortunately, philosophers' inattention to normalcy has meant that the ways of life that define our modern societies have gone largely without defense, even as whole literatures have emerged to condemn them.

Why It's OK: The Ethics and Aesthetics of How We Live seeks to remedy that. It's a series of books that provides accessible, sound, and often new and creative arguments for widespread ethical and aesthetic values. Made up of short volumes that assume no previous knowledge of philosophy from the reader, the series recognizes that philosophy is just as important for understanding what we already believe as it is for criticizing the status quo. The series isn't meant to make us complacent about what we value; rather, it helps and challenges us to think more deeply about the values that give our daily lives meaning.

Titles in Series:

Why It's OK to Speak Your Mind

Hrishikesh Joshi

Why It's OK to Be a Slacker

Alison Suen

Why It's OK to Eat Meat

Dan C. Shahar

Why It's OK to Love Bad Movies

Matthew Strohl

Why It's OK to Not Be Monogamous

Justin L. Clardy

Why It's OK to Trust Science

Keith M. Parsons

Why It's OK to Be a Sports Fan

Alfred Archer and Jake Wojtowicz

Selected Forthcoming Titles:

Why It's OK to Mind Your Own Business

Justin Tosi and Brandon Warmke

Why It's OK to Be Fat

Rekha Nath

Why It's OK to Be a Socialist

Christine Sypnowich

Why It's OK to Be a Moral Failure

Robert B. Talisse

For further information about this series, please visit: www.routledge.com/Why-Its-OK/book-series/WIOK

ALFRED ARCHER AND
JAKE WOJTOWICZ

Why It's OK
to Be a Sports
Fan

Routledge
Taylor & Francis Group
NEW YORK AND LONDON

Designed cover image: Andy Goodman. © Taylor & Francis

First published 2024
by Routledge
605 Third Avenue, New York, NY 10158

and by Routledge
4 Park Square, Milton Park, Abingdon, Oxon, OX14 4RN

Routledge is an imprint of the Taylor & Francis Group, an informa business

ISBN: 978-1-032-22135-9 (hbk)
ISBN: 978-1-032-22134-2 (pbk)
ISBN: 978-1-003-27127-7 (ebk)

DOI: 10.4324/9781003271277

Typeset in Joanna
by Deanta Global Publishing Services, Chennai, India

The Open Access version of this book was funded by Tilburg University Library.

Contents

Acknowledgments

Alfred would like to thank his wife Georgie and their cat Macky for their emotional support during the writing of this book and for putting up with the sudden loud noises when a goal is scored in a match he is watching. Thanks also to those who facilitated my developing fandom as a child: my grandmother Eileen McKay for telling me that I should support Partick Thistle, my parents John Archer and Jenny McKay for taking me to football matches, despite having no interest in football themselves, and my stepfather Simon Frith for taking me to see Partick Thistle despite having no special interest in Thistle or Scottish football. Thanks to all those I have watched football with over the years, especially Mark Crilley, Paul Polson, Micheal Holiday, Liam Young, Laura Bennison, Callum Nelson, Nick Tarlton, Eddie Docherty, Ritchie Phelan, Carlo Garofalo, Nathan Wildman, Matteo Colombo, Seamus Bradley, Rob Smith, Dilan Turkovic, Paris Mavromoustakos Blom and Jack Casey. Thanks also to Benjamin Matheson, with whom I developed much of my thinking about the ethics of admiration, to all my colleagues at Tilburg University for providing such a supportive and encouraging intellectual environment, and to the British Philosophy of Sport Association for helping me to develop my research into the philosophy of sport. Thanks also to the Alexander von Humboldt Foundation for providing a research grant that gave me time to work on this book.

Jake would like to thank his wife Hannah, their dog Archie, and their cat Genny (full name: Gennaro Gattuso) for their love and support. Archie is a keen (if unsophisticated) watcher of almost any ball sport; Genny does not care. Becoming a fan of the Bills with Hannah has been an adventure, and her willingness to become a fan of the England football team – and to support me after the inevitable losses – is much appreciated. Not to mention her patience for all the time I spend watching and thinking about sports, including that one time I woke up at 4am the day before her sister's wedding to watch England beat the Kiwis in the Rugby World Cup semis. Thanks also to my parents, Jan and Jayne Wojtowicz, for taking me to play rugby, often in miserable English weather. It was my first step into enjoying sport and a gateway into fandom. And thanks to all those who have watched or played sport with me, I hope that being a philosopher of sport doesn't make me too much of an annoying companion.

David Papineau and John William Devine ran a wonderful philosophy of sport seminar at King's College London when I was a young grad student that gave me a great insight into how philosophers can talk about sports. Alex Wolf-Root has helped me to think through many important ethical issues in the philosophy of sport. Talking to David Galloway, and seamlessly blending conversations on philosophy and sport, was a highlight of my time at King's College London and made me a better philosopher as well as a better-informed sports fan. Finally, Chris McMullan has helped me think about so many of the interesting things that we find in sport. Without him, I wouldn't understand or appreciate sports anywhere near as well as I do. Thanks also to the Society for Applied Philosophy for a short-term postdoctoral research grant that gave me time to work on parts of this book.

We would both like to thank Nathan Wildman, Kyle Fruh, and Adam Kadlac for talking with us about some of the philosophical issues in this book. Comments from attendees at the British Society for the Philosophy of Sport monthly seminar helped us to work out some of the philosophical questions concerning fandom and community. Other parts of the book benefited from conversations at the British Philosophy of Sport Association 2022, the 2022 Annual Conference of the International Association for Philosophy of Sport, The Second Annual Conference of the Political Science Association's Sport and Politics Group, and the Philosophy of Love Workshop at Tilburg University. Thanks to Alfred's mother Jenny McKay for reading and copyediting the whole manuscript and to the anonymous reviewers of the proposal and manuscript of this book for their encouragement and suggestions. Many thanks also to our editor Andrew Beck for his enthusiasm and editorial help.

On May 15th, 2021, one of the strangest seasons in Scottish soccer history was brought to an end.[1] Due to the COVID-19 pandemic, the entire season had been played without any fans being allowed into the stadiums. In the lower leagues, fans had been made to put up with watching the matches on low-quality streaming services, where the cameras were often operated by artificial intelligence that failed to tell the difference between footballs, seagulls, and the bald heads of assistant referees. In the top league, Glasgow Rangers had blocked the attempt by their fierce rivals Celtic to be champions for the tenth time in a row. An impressive set of performances by Rangers had seen them go undefeated throughout the entire league season.

When Rangers won the title, the country was in the middle of a COVID lockdown. Despite this, thousands of Rangers fans gathered in George Square in Glasgow's city center, where they celebrated by climbing on statues, setting off flares, and singing. In the days that followed, the Rangers fans were roundly criticized by Scottish politicians, health advisors, and newspaper columnists. Rangers fans were not the only sports fans to face this kind of criticism. In England, fans of Premier League winners Liverpool were criticized for breaking lockdown to celebrate; fans of PAOK in Greece were criticized for celebrating their club's 94th anniversary during lockdown;

DOI: 10.4324/9781003271277-1

and fans of Australian rules football were criticized for breaking lockdown rules to celebrate the biggest game of the year. These criticisms are unsurprising; gathering in large numbers to celebrate when most people were following the rules and sacrificing their social lives to help keep infection numbers low was understandably viewed by many as both reckless and selfish.

More surprising, perhaps, was that some media commentators responded by criticizing all soccer fans (not just all Rangers fans) for the actions of a few thousand people. Speaking on BBC Radio Scotland, former newspaper columnist Joan Burnie claimed the problem was soccer (or football, as it is called in the UK) fandom in general. "Football is really a game for a pathetic bunch of losers", she declared before adding that she had "never understood the hold which certain football teams have on the hearts of their supporters".[2] Her complaints were not restricted to the fans, as she then questioned the point of the sport in general. "It is football. It is men kicking a bit of rubber up and down a pitch. ... For goodness' sake, it's a football team. It doesn't matter".[3] Obviously concerned that this nuanced summary might not do justice to the strength of her feelings, she finished by saying: "I would have got out a water cannon, and I would have filled it with disinfectant, and I would have bunged that into George Square and I would have sprayed the lot of them. They are thick".[4]

Burnie's criticism of soccer fans may strike some as too silly to take seriously. The moment when someone advocates spraying bleach in people's faces is usually a good time to stop paying them any attention. But Burnie is far from alone in her negative view of sports fans. Writing in 1912, the social psychologist George Howard described sports fandom as:

A singular example of mental perversion, an absurd and immoral custom tenaciously held fast in mob-mind, has its genesis in the partisan zeal of athletic spectator-crowds. I refer to the practice of organized cheering, known in college argot as "rooting". From every aspect it is bad.[5]

Similarly, the journalist Jim Cummings describes sports fandom as "sad" and "a dangerous waste of time",[6] while the author and philosopher Jorge Luis Borges claimed that "Soccer is popular because stupidity is popular".[7] Meanwhile, the International I Hate Sports Club is a small organization whose goal is "to completely eradicate any trace of sports programming from the public airwaves". Their reason for doing so is that "being addicted to watching sports is abhorrent. We believe that, if people like sports, they should play them, not watch others".[8]

Others see sports fandom as a form of delusional narcissism. In his book *The Culture of Narcissism*, the cultural historian Christopher Lasch argues that fandom serves to "intensify narcissistic dreams of fame and glory" and to "encourage the common man to identify with the stars and to hate the 'herd'". The result of identifying with sporting heroes, according to Lasch, is that it makes it more difficult for ordinary people "to accept the banality of everyday existence".[9] By identifying with sporting heroes, people come to think of themselves as better than others. They are then made to confront the unpleasant truth that their lives do not reflect this view of themselves.

Indeed, as the sports media theorist Noah Cohan argues, sports fans are typically depicted in Hollywood films as "quintessential loser[s]". In films like *Fever Pitch* and *Silver Linings Playbook*, male sports fans are presented as childlike failures who have failed to accept the realities of adult life. For example, in the American version of *Fever Pitch* (there is a British version, too, based on Nick Hornby's book about his love for the soccer team Arsenal), Ben Wrightman is a math teacher and obsessive Red Sox fan who is in a relationship with corporate executive Lindsey Meeks. As Cohan describes, Ben is presented as "a fool, a teacher with less maturity than the young minds he purports to mold".[10] He turns down opportunities to meet Lindsey's parents or go on a romantic weekend to Paris, preferring to go to see the Red Sox instead. In a telling scene, Lindsey jokes that Ben's clothes are not the kind of clothes an adult man should wear, leading her to say to him, "You're like a man-boy! Half man, half boy". To this, Ben replies: "sometimes I like to be 11 years old". As Cohan summarizes, "the message is clear: Ben is an overgrown child".[11] Sports fandom, it seems, is fine for children but is not an appropriate pastime for a real adult.

Despite these criticisms and unflattering media portrayals, being a sports fan is incredibly popular. According to a recent poll (conducted in 2022), 70% of Americans describe themselves as sports fans, and 26% of Americans describe themselves as *avid* fans.[12] Are all these fans engaging in something juvenile? Are they all idiots, narcissists, or adults who refuse to grow up?

As committed sports fans, we have both found ourselves struggling with these questions. We find these questions all the more pressing given that we both have PhDs in moral philosophy, the academic discipline that studies what it is to live a good life. If sports fandom is a waste of time, then it looks like we have both dedicated large parts of our professional lives to studying what makes a life go well and dedicated large parts of our free time to a hobby that makes no contribution to a well-lived life. This would certainly be a disappointing conclusion to draw!

Thankfully, though, we are convinced that sports fandom can play a valuable role in people's lives, and our aim in this book is to persuade you of this. Though we don't expect to persuade everybody, we want to try to get those of you who hate sports fandom to see that there are some good things about being a sports fan. And we also want to equip fans so that they can fight back when confronted by, say, snobbish academics sneering at "sportsball" and arguing that fandom is some idiotic waste of time. But we also recognize that there are some genuine serious issues with being a fan – and we want to suggest a few ways that fans might face these issues.

We will do this by first exploring what sports fandom is and then responding to the various different reasons why people think that it is not OK to be a sports fan.

In Chapter 1, we will explore the nature of sports fandom by arguing that sports fandom is a form of love. Like romantic love, sports fandom involves an appreciation of particular qualities, practices that express and foster attachment, and changes to our perception. This may be a love of a particular player, a team, or a whole sport.

Viewing fandom as a form of love leads us to the first reason to question sports fandom. When romantic love goes well, it leads to real relationships between human beings that can play an important role in a meaningful and valuable life. But sports fandom might be thought to contribute nothing to such a life. Someone may love the Red Sox, but the Red Sox will not love them back. How, then, can such a one-sided form of love contribute to a well-lived life? In Chapter 2, we will respond to this objection by exploring the many ways in which sports fandom can make a positive contribution to our lives. Fandom can make us happy, provide a useful outlet through which to manage our emotions, bring people together into a community, and help us develop a sense of identity. In doing so, fandom can make an important contribution to a meaningful life. While there are many other pursuits that might provide similar benefits, sports fandom also has some more distinctive contributions to make to our lives. It helps to teach us about how to live a good life, and sports have their own aesthetic values, which fandom allows us to appreciate.

Although there are ways in which fandom can make a positive contribution to our lives, we might still wonder whether it is the kind of hobby that sensible adults would devote their time to. Specifically, we might worry about *partisan fans*, those who are devoted fans of particular teams, as opposed to *purists*, who love the sport but are neutrals when it comes to particular teams. Aren't partisan fans simply man-boys (or woman-girls) who have failed to properly grow up, like Ben from *Fever Pitch*? In Chapter 3, we will consider a version of this worry, which holds that partisans do not *really* believe that the results of sport matches matter but are instead engaging in a form of make-believe in which they are pretending that the result matters. This, we might think, is not the kind of activity that sensible adults would devote large portions of their free time to. Relatedly, we might worry that whatever benefits can be gained from watching sports will not be available to those who watch in the biased and one-sided way that partisans do. We will defend partisans against both of these objections. First, we will argue that many partisans are not engaging in make-believe; the results really do matter to them. This is because they are part of a community – a community of fans – and the whole point of this community is that it succeeds when its team wins. Next, we will argue that while it is true that partisan fans will miss out on some of the benefits of watching sport available to purists, partisans are also able to appreciate the drama of sports matches more intensely than neutrals. Both purist and partisan ways of watching sport, then, have their benefits.

But this is not the only criticism that is leveled against partisans. When partisans are not criticized for being childish, they may find themselves criticized for being adversarial hooligans. Partisan fandom is criticized for encouraging hatred and anger towards rival fan groups. In Chapter 4, we accept that there is something to this criticism. At its worst, partisan fandom can lead to intense hatred of rivals, particularly when sporting opposition builds on and feeds existing tensions between different groups. However, it can also lead to positive acts of solidarity and altruism. Like many other powerful forces in society, such as love and religion, fandom can encourage both good and bad behavior. Moreover, committed partisan fandom is both a form of loyalty and a way of developing a more general virtue of loyalty. While it is true that this loyalty can sometimes develop into worrying forms of adversarial behavior, it can also play a valuable role in a well-lived life.

This, though, raises another issue for partisan fans. When should they abandon their commitment to their team or their fellow fans? In Chapters 5 and 6, we will consider these issues by examining how fans ought to respond when either their fellow fans or the club that they love behaves despicably. How should fans respond when their fellow fans act in violent, racist, or sexist ways? How should fans respond when the club or athletes they love act terribly? While our aim in this book is to persuade you that it is OK to be a sports fan, this fandom comes with ethical responsibilities. We will argue that fans should be *critical fans*. This form of fandom combines loyalty towards the athlete, team, or sport one is a fan of with the ability to treat one's fandom with a critical eye. In some cases, this may involve attempting to change your team or fellow fans for the better. In extreme cases, it may involve walking away from your fandom altogether.

Being a sports fan is OK … but it is not always OK.

Fandom: What's love got to do with it?

1

In a typical National Football League (NFL) season, fans of the Houston Texans each spend on average $380 on merchandise, while fans of the Cleveland Browns and the LA Rams also spend over $300.[1] Even the lowest-spending NFL fans, the Indianapolis Colts, spend an average of $85 each year on merchandise. When it comes to food and drink, Buffalo Bills fans spend around $125 on food and $60 on drink for their entire party at each match, while fans of the Texans spend around the same on drink and top the list on food, spending a whopping $170 on food per match. The lowest spenders, fans of Carolina Panthers, still spend a combined $60 on food and drink. And this is just the money spent in-stadium; it doesn't include the money spent on tickets or travel, and it doesn't account for the beer, chicken wings, or TV subscription packages fans pay for when they watch at home.

Turning from American football to English soccer, "dedicated fans" – fans who attend every home Premier League match and at least five away games – spend an average of £1,888 per person each year on supporting their team. This is "8% of the average UK take home salary".[2] If fans were to attend every one of their team's Premier League away games, they would travel an average of over 5,000 miles. There won't be many fans who go to every game, but some will, and the distances traveled can be huge.

DOI: 10.4324/9781003271277-2

Some fans go even further and are willing to give over (parts of) their bodies for fandom, covering their bodies in team tattoos.[3] For others, "till death do us part" isn't enough, and they are buried in coffins adorned with their club's badge and colors.[4]

Fans of individual athletes also go to great lengths to show their devotion. Many Roger Federer fans have his name or image tattooed on their bodies. Other fans want to have a piece of their favorite player's body for themselves, like Karen Shemonsky, who in 1999 paid $8,000 to buy the dentures of baseball great Ty Cobb.[5] Other fans express their devotion through the names of their children, like Alyssa and Dan Hoven, fans of the St Louis Blues ice hockey team, who named their son Vlad after their favorite player, Vladimir Tarasenko.[6]

Clearly, sports fandom plays a very important role in the lives of many people – even though, as we saw in the Introduction, many others find this ridiculous. But what is it about sports fandom that inspires these forms of devotion? In this chapter, we will answer this question by exploring the nature of sports fandom. We will argue that sports fandom is a form of love. We'll start by explaining the various ways in which sports fandom is similar to love, before going further and arguing that fandom is not only *like* love, it *is* love, or at least a version of it. However, not all sports fandom is the same; some sports fans love a particular club, while others love the game itself or particular athletes. We'll look at the different forms that sports fandom can take and explain why each is still a form of love.

But love can make us do bad things. It can make us join in on awful, racist chants; it can make us care for our team at the expense of doing the right thing; it can make us violent and lead us to become the kind of people we would rather not be.

This chapter is just about understanding how love and fandom relate – we'll get on to these problems shortly.

1.1 TWO LOVE STORIES

Let's start with a love story. James and Mary were 18 when they first met. From this first meeting, James was captivated by Mary's intelligence, sense of humor, and beauty. He found himself thinking about her for long periods every day and counting down the hours until he could see her again. They started dating and quickly fell in love. James felt that he had met the person who he wanted to spend his life with. As he fell more deeply in love, he started to view everything about Mary in an ever more positive light. While he might concede that it was possible that there might be other people who were more beautiful, intelligent, or funny than Mary, it was Mary's beauty, intelligence, and humor that he loved. They got married within a year and organized a large wedding for all their friends and family. As James got older, he often had to travel for his job. When on the road, he would call Mary every day and always make sure to bring her back a gift from wherever he had been. While James and Mary both changed significantly as they grew older, their love survived, and they stayed together their whole lives.

Compare this to a different kind of story. Alfred's first experience of watching soccer live was a match between Partick Thistle and Motherwell when he was eight years old. He immediately became enthralled by the excitement of the match, the passion of the players, and the humor of the fans. He soon became an avid fan and would go to every match that he could persuade his parents to take him to. When he was old enough to start going to matches by himself, he started following his team to away matches as well, traveling all over

Scotland on supporters' buses to watch them. Wherever he went, he and his fellow fans would sing that Partick Thistle "are by far the greatest team, the world has ever seen". If pushed, he would concede that all the available evidence would suggest that this was not, in fact, the case. In fact, they were not even the best team the Scottish Second Division had seen that season. Nevertheless, Thistle were his team, and he found himself thinking about them regularly, working out what team they should field for the next match, replaying goals in his head, and scouring the internet for rumors about their latest transfer targets. While the players and managers changed regularly, Alfred's support remained constant.

While these stories are unlikely to win any writing awards, they do present an initial similarity between loving a person and loving a sports team. But what exactly do love and being a sports fan have in common?

1.2 APPRECIATION OF PARTICULAR QUALITIES[7]

One important feature of many loving relationships is that we love someone for the individual person that they are. The philosopher Robert Nozick claims that when we first fall in love with someone, we may be impressed by the positive qualities they possess, just as James was impressed by Mary's intelligence, humor, and beauty.[8] However, as this love develops, it changes from being a response to these admirable qualities into an appreciation of the unique way that the loved one embodies these properties. This explains why love may survive the loss or change of the qualities that led us to fall in love with someone in the first place, as our love has focused on the special identity of the person, not just their impressive qualities. It also explains why people are reluctant to "trade up" their beloved when they meet someone who is funnier and more beautiful, as our love is not just an appreciation of beauty and humor but of this particular beauty and this particular humor.

This was the case with James, in the story in the previous section, whose initial admiration for Mary's qualities developed into an appreciation of the particular way in which Mary was intelligent, beautiful, and funny. Over time, James's appreciation of Mary's humor shifts to a focus on the particular way in which Mary is funny, the way she tells her jokes, and the widening of her eyes when she reaches the punchline. He loves her not just because she is kind, but because of the way in which this kindness is expressed through caring for lost and injured animals. The fact that it is these qualities that James appreciates explains why he would not leave Mary even if he met a woman funnier, cleverer, and more beautiful than Mary. This person may be wonderful in many ways, even more wonderful than Mary, but she is not wonderful in the way that Mary is wonderful. It may also explain why James's love survives the way that Mary changes over time, as his love is focused on Mary as a person, not just her impressive qualities.

The philosopher Nicholas Dixon makes a similar comparison between sports fandom and love.[9] Sports fandom may begin with an appreciation of the wonderful features of a team or an athlete but over time, is likely to develop into a love of the particular way in which they display these qualities. The Buffalo Bills play with a certain grit and determination, but also with genuine levels of joy, set against decades of failure; FC Barcelona play with a particular style that goes back nearly half a century. A fan of a sports team will not simply trade in their team when another team starts to display higher levels of skill or begins to win more matches. Rather, their fandom will continue even if the team loses some of the qualities that attracted the fan to this team in the first place. The best players may move on, but the love of the team will remain. As with romantic love, fandom involves an attachment to something in particular, rather than an appreciation of abstract qualities.

We may even question whether someone can count as a fan of a team if they are willing to switch their team as soon as that team starts performing badly.[10] But this doesn't mean that fans must stick with their team no matter what. If a team loses all of the qualities that attracted the fan to them in the first place, then it may make sense for the fan to stop loving them. And if your team becomes morally awful, as we'll explore in the second half of this book, that might also be a good reason to leave your team. Much like a romantic break-up, that can be heartbreaking.

1.3 PRACTICES OF ATTACHMENT

Another way in which sports fandom resembles love is that both involve social practices designed both to express and to strengthen attachment. Lovers often participate in a range of cultural practices that help to make it clear how they feel about each other. James and Mary, for example, began with the relatively informal practice of dating and introducing each other to their friends and family before moving onto more formal practices such as marriage and buying a home together. Even after making such big commitments, James maintains smaller practices such as buying Mary gifts whenever he is traveling to help display his love for her. These practices may vary significantly for people from different cultures.

Even within the same culture, different people may participate in some practices but not others and may also develop their own unique ways of strengthening their relationship. Some people go to the cinema together once a week, others take big trips once a year; some people like to eat fancy meals together, others go on walks. Some people think marriage is an important practice for signaling commitment to each other and to friends and family, while other people find this practice unnecessary. Whatever practices lovers engage in, we can see that when these practices go well, they allow lovers to show to themselves and others how they feel about each other and by doing so, to bring them closer together.

Sports fandom also involves social practices that enable fans to express their attachment to the team. Erin Tarver, for example, describes how as a young fan of the LSU Tigers football team, she would study the sports pages before going to school in the morning, collect LSU merchandise, learn the songs her fellow fans sang in the stadium, and seek out creative ways to display the team colors on her body with nail polish and temporary tattoos.[11] As the sociologist Richard Giulianotti argues, sports fandom involves elements of ritual, which have much in common with religious ceremonies.[12] Sports matches take place in places that fans hold to have "sacred qualities", matches and seasons follow distinctive rhythms, fans dress in the appropriate ceremonial clothing (team jerseys), and all of this helps to build a strong sense of community between the fans. Fans also show off how much they know about their club and test the knowledge of their fellow fans. The economist Kevin Quinn has argued that these kinds of practices help fans to strengthen their attachment to their team in much the same way that religious practices help people to strengthen their religious feelings. As he puts it: "Going to church becomes more meaningful as church attendance becomes more frequent. Similarly, the time that a fan spends following the local team today results in greater enjoyment when following the team tomorrow".[13] These rituals play an important role in expressing the commitment of fans to the team and solidarity with their fellow fans.[14] Like love, fandom is far from passive.

1.4 PERCEPTION

Love changes how we perceive the world. When we fall in love with someone, we see them differently from how we did before. As James fell in love with Mary, she started to occupy a more central part of his world. As the philosopher Troy Jollimore describes it, love is "largely a matter of paying close attention to a person".[15] The more attention we pay to the person we love, the less attention we are likely to pay to other people. Love, then, involves a shift in our attention towards the person we love and away from others.[16]

Love not only changes how much attention we pay to someone; it also changes how we perceive them. When we fall in love with someone, we start to see them in a more positive light. This means paying more attention to their positive qualities and focusing less on their less positive qualities. It may involve taking a more sympathetic or understanding approach to their faults or even overlooking them altogether.[17] Falling in love with Mary is likely to make it harder for James to perceive the flaws Mary may have and to take a more generous attitude towards those he does perceive. Love also makes us see the world in a way that is closer to how the person we love views the world. Someone who falls in love with a ballet enthusiast may come to find something valuable in ballet that they had not seen before, as they begin to see it in a way that more closely resembles the way the person they love perceives it.

No doubt this sounds familiar to those of you who know sports fans. Being a sports fan changes our perceptions in similar ways. When Alfred became a fan of Partick Thistle, he started paying close attention to their results and their latest signings. When reading the sports section of the newspaper, he immediately reads any stories about his team before even looking at the rest. When watching a match, he pays far more attention to how Thistle are performing than the performance of the opposition and often will not be able to remember who scored the opposition's goals. While Alfred is willing to concede that Partick Thistle may not be the greatest team the world has ever seen, he continually overestimates how they will do each year. Major flaws with the team, such as a lack of width, the over-reliance on one striker to score all the goals, and the lack of a ball-winning midfielder, are dismissed as overly pessimistic worries that will be no barrier to success.

Being a fan also changes how Alfred perceives refereeing decisions. For some reason, referees always seem to favor the opposition and consistently make mistakes that go against his team. The philosopher Stephen Mumford explains this phenomenon by saying that unlike neutral observers, a team's supporters view the match through the lens of "competitive interest".[18] By this, he means that the events on the field will be viewed from the point of view of their impact on the outcome of the contest. When a fan's team concedes a last-minute goal, it will not simply be seen as a tidy finish or a defensive lapse but rather, as a tragedy. When the referee makes a borderline decision against their team, the fan will view this as an outrageous error made by someone who is obviously biased towards the opposition. (This characterization is at least broadly true, though in Chapter 3, we'll argue that things are a bit more nuanced than this.) In other words, fans are viewing the game from the perspective of their team, in much the same way that lovers might see the world through the eyes of their beloved.

1.5 FANDOM AS LOVE

These similarities between fandom and love give us good reason to view fandom as one form of love. Some may find this idea odd. Love, they might claim, involves a mutual relationship between two people. According to some views of love, this relationship is crucial. The philosopher Niko Kolodny, for example, claims that love involves valuing a personal relationship that you have with another person.[19] In the case of sports fandom, however, we might think that the relationship will be entirely one-way. The team or the athlete may influence the fan's view of the world, but the fan is unlikely to have any influence in return. If this is right, then it casts doubt on the analogy of fandom as love, as fandom would involve a different form of identification from other kinds of love.

We have two responses to this objection. First, the relationship between sports fans and the teams or athletes they admire is not entirely one-way. In his study of fandom, the media studies scholar Cornel Sandvoss explains how fans not only respond to those they are a fan of but also project their own selves onto those they support. They "superimpose attributes of the self, their beliefs and value systems and, ultimately, their sense of self on the object of fandom".[20] The way in which fans project their own selves is likely to have at least some impact on the self-conception of their idols. The way that fans of Lebron James respond to him will have some impact on how he thinks of himself. The case is even more plausible where sports teams are concerned. This is because there is good reason to think that the identity of a sports team is at least partly constituted by its fans, as several philosophers of sports have argued.[21] Fans help to lend an atmosphere to a stadium, they have favorite players, and they insist a team plays in a certain style, shaping a team's commitment to certain principles over decades. For instance, when Barcelona or Ajax resort to long-ball football, or when Manchester United fail to attack with enough energy, fans make their displeasure clear.

Second, there is also good reason to think that love does not always involve a mutual shaping of identities. If it did, then unrequited love could not count as a genuine form of love, as the target of this love may not be influenced in any way by the person who is in love with them. While unrequited love can be unpleasant for both the lover and the person who cannot return the love, there is no reason to think that this is not real love.[22] If this is right, then it would be a mistake to think that love must involve a mutual relationship between two people. The kind of love involved in fandom may be closer to unrequited love than to the kind of love that exists in a romantic partnership, but this does not give us reason to think that it is not a form of love.

Another worry we might have is that love is an emotion we have towards other people. Going back to Kolodny's view, love is a response to a *personal* relationship, so it only makes sense to love other people.[23] This is no problem for fandom that concerns a particular person, such as fandom for Usain Bolt or Lebron James. However, it does raise a problem for the idea that being a fan of a sports club could be a form of love. This form of love is not focused on a person but on a collective entity. This may be enough to persuade some people that this form of fandom cannot be a genuine form of love.

However, limiting love to other human beings is too restrictive. First, there is good reason to think that we can love non-human animals, as any pet lover will know.[24] Second, people may love objects, such as the book they have dedicated their life to writing or the house they grew up in.[25] More relevant for our purposes is that patriotism may be understood as a form of love, the love for one's country. According to philosopher Martha Nussbaum, loving one's country involves loving a collective entity that one identifies with.[26] In fact, in making her case for this, Nussbaum compares the love of one's country with the love of a sports team. In both cases, Nussbaum says that love involves strong feelings of identification with the object of love. Both sports fans and patriots feel that they belong to their country or their team and also that the team or country belongs to them. They feel part of a "we", a collective entity made up of their fellow fans or citizens. If we accept that we can love collectives like countries, then it also makes sense to think that we can love sports teams.

So, it seems that love that is not directed towards persons can be a genuine form of love. There does not seem to be any good reason on this front, then, to think that we cannot love sports teams.

1.6 VARIETIES OF FANDOM

We have argued that fandom is not just similar to love in some ways but should also be considered a form of love. But it might be pointed out that up to now, we have only been thinking about one kind of sports fan: the fan who is a committed supporter of one particular team or athlete. These fans, known as *partisans*, do not simply watch for the love of sport; they have an attachment to particular competitors and want them to succeed over the others.[27] Partisans can come in stronger and weaker varieties. An extreme partisan may follow their team home and away, get the club's badge tattooed on their body, and be incapable of appreciating the abilities of any team apart from their own. They will support their team through thick and thin. No matter how badly the team is performing, the extreme partisan will be there in the stands cheering them on. More mild partisans will have a clear preference for their team, may go to see them play a few times a year, but still be able to appreciate beautiful goals or touchdowns that are scored against their team. They will certainly be there to see their team play in a cup final or to win the league. However, when the team stops performing well, they may find they have better ways to fill their time.

Alfred is a soccer partisan and can be found somewhere between the extreme and the moderate. He regularly goes to support his team when they play at home but rarely goes to away matches. He finds it much easier to appreciate beautiful play from his team than from the opposition but has been known to grudgingly applaud a particularly excellent bit of skill from opposition players. These kinds of fans fit easily with the idea that sports fandom is a form of love, as they are attached to particular teams or athletes, and they care about them in ways that alter their perception.

But not all fans are partisans. Some fans, purists, are fans of the sport itself but have no allegiance to any competitor.[28] Take Jake, for example, who is not a fan of any particular soccer team but devotes hours every week to watching soccer. When Jake is watching a game, he is not rooting for a particular team to win (with one big exception: when England are playing); he simply wants to see an interesting and exciting game with a beautiful goal or two. He can easily appreciate the game no matter who wins. While he occasionally develops a fondness for a particular player, like Paul Scholes, this is simply an appreciation of the beautiful way that they play rather than a desire for that player to succeed over others.

On the face of it, purists might not seem to fit easily with the idea that fandom is a form of love. After all, the purist is not attached to a particular team that they care deeply about; rather, they simply enjoy watching talented players play a sport well. We might think, then, that their attitude is closer to admiration rather than love, as they appreciate high-level performance rather than showing committed support for particular competitors. However, as we understand the purist, they do have particular commitments and attachments, but these are directed towards particular sports rather than particular teams or athletes. Take Jake's love for soccer. From a pure time point of view, he spends far more time watching soccer than many partisans do. His love for soccer certainly influences his perception; as he fell in love with soccer, it came to occupy an increasingly large proportion of his attention. When the sports news is on TV, he always pays closer attention to the soccer news than to other sports. He also finds his attention drawn consistently to the positive qualities of soccer, even as he learns more about the dark side of the beautiful game. Jake's fandom is a form of love, though it is love for the game rather than love of a team.

The strength of attachment to a particular team or athlete is not the only difference to be found among sports fans. The sociologist Richard Giulianotti argues that we can also distinguish between different kinds of attachment that people have to a team.[29] *Traditional* fans are those with a strong cultural attachment to a team, who cheer the team on in the stadium. This attachment may be a local one. Many fans start supporting the team closest to them, as this is the team that represents their town or city. The connection may also be historical.

Children often inherit their fandom from their parents, even if the family no longer lives quite so close by. Other cultural reasons may also inform this identification. In Glasgow, Scotland, for example, there is one soccer club with a strong Roman Catholic identity (Glasgow Celtic) and another with a strongly Protestant identity (Glasgow Rangers). Here, religious identity plays a major factor in determining which team people support. Moreover, many Catholics from far beyond Glasgow feel a close cultural connection to Celtic and, as a result, have a strong emotional connection to the club and travel regularly to see them. For example, The Naomh Padraig Celtic Supporters Club is based in Dublin, Ireland, and organizes trips for fans to make the long journey by bus and ferry to Glasgow for Celtic's home matches. Buses typically leave at 3:45am to make it to Glasgow for 3pm kick-off. While these fans may not live close to their team, they go to great lengths to make sure they are there in the stadium.

But not all sports fans have this kind of connection with a team. Some have more of a consumer relationship with their team. These fans may not be able to attend the team's matches but spend significant sums of money on fan merchandise and on television subscriptions to see their games. They may identify strongly with the team, but this identification is not informed by any local or cultural affinity. While the team may play a significant role in the identity of these fans, these fans do not play a major role in determining the identity of the club. When people think of Celtic fans, for example, they tend to think of those who turn up to the stadium and create the world-famous atmosphere, rather than those watching at home on TV. While this distinction between traditional and consumerist forms of fandom is interesting and important, in the remainder of the book we're mostly going to be focusing on the difference between purists and partisans, as this is the distinction that is most important for our purposes.

1.7 CONCLUSION

We have argued that sports fandom is a form of love and that this goes for both partisan and purist forms of fandom. We might wonder, though, whether one of these forms of fandom is superior to the other. Is Jake's appreciation of soccer a purer and more virtuous form of fandom than Alfred's loyal commitment to a team? Does Alfred's commitment to Partick Thistle show that he really loves his team, whereas Jake is merely entertained by soccer but could never understand the love Alfred feels? While these are natural questions to ask, we think that there is no need to rank one as superior to the other. Most fans will lie somewhere on the spectrum between the partisan and the purist, and this position is likely to change in different situations. Alfred, for example, is a fierce partisan when watching Partick Thistle or Willem II but enjoys watching the English Premier League as a purist, more interested in seeing an exciting game than in who wins. Jake, on the other hand, is a purist when it comes to club soccer but a partisan when it comes to international soccer and the Buffalo Bills.

The experiences of each of these fans have something to be said for them. The purist is able to enjoy an exciting match no matter who wins, while the partisan will likely be distraught to see their team lose an excellent game at a crucial point of the season. The partisan, on the other hand, will be able to enjoy games that are not particularly high in skill or beauty. One of Alfred's favorite games as a Willem II fan, for example, was when they beat local rivals PSV Eindhoven 2-1 despite having only one shot on target (the other was an own goal). Both the Willem II goals were the result of defensive mistakes rather than attacking skill, and neither team offered a great deal of exciting play or impressive talent. Nevertheless, for the Willem II fans, this was an incredible match, as they had beaten their far bigger and more successful rivals.

We will return to the discussion of the comparative merits of partisan and purist forms of fandom in Chapter 3. For now, we simply wish to make an initial case for the idea that both forms of fandom can be valuable ways of appreciating sport. As we will see in the chapters that follow, substantial objections have been raised against both forms of fandom, especially partisan fandom. Our aim will be to persuade you that though many of these objections should be taken seriously, it is nevertheless OK to be a sports fan. We will begin this defense in the next chapter, where we will explain why being a sports fan is not a waste of time.

As we've seen, fans spend a lot of time and effort on their sports. They can be utterly fanatical, look like narcissists or little kids to outsiders, spend a ton of money, and sometimes do incredibly odd things (like being buried in team coffins) because of their fandom. They do this because they are in love.

But this love isn't just for odd extremists. We like to think we're relatively well-adjusted human beings, not absolute sport freaks. But consider the time and money that we, the authors, spend on sports fandom. Alfred supports two soccer teams, Partick Thistle in Scotland and Willem II in the Netherlands. He spends hours every week on these fandoms: reading news and fan forums, listening to podcasts and radio programs, and watching highlights and live matches. He spends 300 euros per year on a season ticket to Willem II, even though he knows he will miss many of the games. During the COVID-19 pandemic, when lockdown rules meant fans were not allowed into the stadium to watch the games, he even turned down the opportunity for a refund on a ticket he had been virtually unable to use. He also regularly spends 15 euros or more on low-quality streams of badly filmed Partick Thistle matches. On top of this, he is also a fan of soccer as a sport more generally and spends yet more hours listening to soccer podcasts, reading soccer news and books, and watching the biggest matches of the week.

DOI: 10.4324/9781003271277-3

Jake isn't a fan of any soccer team but puts in a lot of effort to watch matches since moving from England to the USA. He will organize his week to watch Champions League matches (which start at 3pm for him) and wake up early on a Saturday for Premier League games. Like Alfred, he spends hours every week listening to those same podcasts and reading articles and books to keep up with what's happening on the other side of the Atlantic. He also, somehow, convinced his American wife, Hannah, to become a soccer fan, and now she will avidly cheer for England with him (and join him in his jaunts to the local English-owned bar). When England played New Zealand in the 2019 Rugby World Cup semi-finals, he was in Columbus, Ohio for a wedding. He woke up at 4am and made a small tent with a bedsheet and a chair in the corner of his room so he could watch at the lowest possible volume without waking the long-suffering Hannah (who eventually joined to watch a fantastic game) or the rest of her family. He has also recently become a fan of the Buffalo Bills and avidly watches them, trying to learn the sport from scratch.

We are not alone in investing time, money, and effort in watching sports. In her wonderful book *Baseball Life Advice*, journalist Stacey May Fowles outlines how her love for baseball and the men who play it (the boys of summer) determines how she spends her time:

> Since 2011, the boys of summer have come to dictate how I navigate most of my days, even the ones during the long, dark offseason when diamonds [baseball fields] across North America are piled with snow. I scour the news for their stories daily, these strangers who've devoted their lives to a child's game. I've learned how former Toronto Blue Jay Mark Buehrle loves his pit bulls, how Texas Ranger Josh Hamilton bounced back from

drug and alcohol addictions, how Seattle Mariner Adam Lind's wife is from Scarborough, Ontario. I check up on the stats of my favorite hitters and pitchers, sneak game updates on my phone at social events, and cultivate a small community of similar devotees to share stories with.[1]

The way Fowles structures her time around her fandom is likely to strike a chord with many sports fans. To the confusion of those who do not share our love of sport, we sports fans dedicate significant portions of our time, income, and attention to our obsession.

But isn't this all a waste of time? Wouldn't it be better to spend this time developing our own talents rather than watching athletes display theirs? Shouldn't we instead spend this time catching up on the work we are behind with, giving our houses a long-overdue clean, or tending to our much-neglected gardens? Or perhaps, we could spend this time catching up with friends and family or having romantic evenings with our partners. Wouldn't it be more meaningful to become a better lover, friend, or family member than to watch another 90 minutes of soccer?

The soccer journalist Barry Glendenning summed this up by saying: "Football is not particularly important in the cosmic scheme of things. People are ill, people are worried about work and how they are going to pay for things and in that regard football doesn't amount to a hill of beans".[2] Glendenning was speaking early in the COVID-19 pandemic, at a time where we were forced to reevaluate what was important to us. But such doubts precede the pandemic. For many people, sports fandom is, at best, a waste of time. At worst, it is destructive, causing people to do awful things for no good reason.

As keen sports fans, we are used to hearing such criticisms and to being gently mocked for our interest in "sportsball".

(There are many legitimate criticisms of fandom – that's the whole point of this book – but sometimes it is important to remember what drives some people in their antipathy: snobbery.) We understand that the life of a sports fan looks quite strange to those who have never been fans themselves. But we think that these criticisms miss the valuable role that sports fandom plays in the lives of so many people. Some forms of love might be a waste of time, but we will argue that among other things, sports fandom can make our lives more meaningful. It's OK to take no interest in sport, but it's also OK to be a dedicated sports fan.

To get to this point, we want to take on two forms of the objection to fandom. The first is that watching sports is just a waste of time; against this, we'll argue it makes us happy, brings us together, and even shapes our identities in a way that can play an important part of a meaningful life. The second objection comes out of these benefits. It's that the benefits that come with fandom have nothing to do with sport, and we could have fun, and get some meaning in our lives, by joining a book club or going to the theater. But we think this is wrong, too. We'll argue that sports have qualities that teach us how to live a good life, and sports have their own aesthetic qualities that we can't get elsewhere.

2.1 WATCHING SPORTS IS A WASTE OF TIME

2.1.1 Fandom makes us happy

Why might watching sport be worthwhile? A helpful starting point here can be found in Fowles's description of how watching baseball makes her feel:

> The emotion the game stirs in me is like an itch I can't scratch, a feeling I'll never really understand. The closest

I've gotten is likening it to a brand-new crush that doesn't fade as the years pass – forever unrequited, deep-bone affection that spurs me onward instead of demoralizing me. Most of the time, I'm simply happy that I care about something that much.[3]

What Fowles is describing here is a form of love: a deep affection, similar to a crush, that brings her joy. Baseball makes her happy.

Perhaps it is not surprising that someone like Fowles, who decided to write a book about fandom, enjoys being a fan. After all, if she didn't enjoy fandom, she might find a more enjoyable topic to write about. Some people, though, may find this claim surprising. Anyone who has sat through a close and important match with a dedicated sports fan may think that they look anything but happy. Are the pained expressions when a team concedes a goal or touchdown really the look of someone who is happy? Would someone who is happy really spend their time shouting at professional athletes from the stands or even more bizarrely, from their sofa while watching TV? When a fan is brought to tears by their team facing relegation or going out of the play-offs, they appear to be anything but happy.

But Fowles is far from alone in finding fandom to be a source of happiness. Indeed, a growing body of evidence suggests that fandom has a positive effect on happiness and well-being. Researchers have found that those who identify closely with a sports team experience lower levels of alienation,[4] lower levels of loneliness,[5] and higher levels of positive emotions and well-being.[6] As psychologist Daniel Wann summarizes his decades of research into sports fandom, "Sport fandom is positively associated with psychological well-being, and the association is likely causal".[7] Being a fan is likely why they are happy. Or, as journalist Larry Olmsted puts more simply, "Sports fans are happier people".[8] But why is this the case? What is it about being a sports fan that makes people happier?

2.1.2 Fandom helps us deal with our emotions

One way that fandom can make us happier is in helping us deal with our emotions. According to the sociologists Norbert Elias and Eric Dunning, sport plays a crucial role in modern societies, as it allows us a space to experience excitement. They argue that modern societies provide few opportunities for people to experience and express intense emotions. Many of the crises that humans faced in the past, such as famines and floods, have been all but eradicated, while others, such as the threats posed by violence and disease, have been significantly reduced (Elias and Dunning were writing long before anyone had heard of COVID-19 and before the climate crisis became so prominent). While these are welcome developments, they also make it less likely that we will feel the intense emotions that these crises are likely to provoke. At the same time, people's emotions have also been subject to greater forms of control:

> Uncontrolled and uncontrollable outbreaks of strong communal excitement in public and even in private have become less frequent. Individual people who act in a highly excited manner are liable to be taken to hospital or to prison. The social and personal organization of excitement control, for containing passionate excitement in public and even in private, has become stronger and more effective.[9]

The increased control of intense emotions helps people to live in harmony with one another. However, it also presents a problem, they argue, as people have a need for excitement and the intense emotional experiences that accompany it.[10] A modern society may be at risk of "dulling the life of its members"[11] and may even present a threat to mental health.[12]

Happily, though, sports and other forms of leisure activities create a space where these emotions can be expressed more freely. Sports offer an opportunity for the "pleasurable de-controlling of human feelings",[13] which Elias and Dunning describe as a form of "emotional refreshment".[14] In other words, they provide us with a space where we can experience and freely express intense emotions that are usually discouraged in modern life.

Sports fandom can also help us deal with our emotions in other ways, by being an important source of solace in times of loss or trauma. Journalist Charlie Morris describes how his support of his local soccer club, Crewe Alexandria, was an important source of comfort to him following the death of his mother when he was a child: "Football had already become a happy zone that I jumped into at every opportunity but now it also offered an exit from sorrow. Life had turned bleak yet football could transport me out of it, not just at matches but through thinking about it".[15] Similarly, soccer fan Heather describes to journalist Peter Ross how she rediscovered her fandom after a bad break-up: "We split up, and it was a place where I could go back to and felt, 'This is where I belong'".[16]

For Stacey Fowles, being a baseball fan was crucial to her recovery from depression and trauma. A traumatic experience when Fowles was a teenager led to a range of mental health problems including claustrophobia, agoraphobia, anxiety, and depression. She tried various ways of treating these problems, from psychiatry and drugs to mindfulness and acupuncture. The one consistent source of comfort that Fowles was able to find was baseball fandom: "Through it all, the one thing that has buoyed me is baseball: its tiny dramas, its compelling backstories, its Powerade victories, its hot, sweaty midsummer slumps".[17] In her experience, she is far from alone in this:

> Without exaggeration, I have had fans tell me that baseball saved them when they most needed saving – during break-ups, health crises, mental health struggles, and grief – and that it gave them something to hold on to when there was nothing else to be found. The game provides the communal structure that so many of us desperately need when we feel isolated and untethered, and invokes a faith we sometimes can't otherwise muster in our daily lives.[18]

Far from being a waste of time, then, sports fandom is capable of providing not only excitement to those who need it but also comfort and stability to those enduring difficult times. At times when life is in turmoil, fandom can offer escapism, but it can also offer a reassuringly constant presence and provide a crucial sense of stability and belonging.

This last point was abundantly clear in the early stages of the COVID-19 pandemic. With many professional sports matches canceled, many of us simply did not know what to do with our free time. As the author John Lanchester describes, "the absence of sport created a hole in my life, a gap in time, especially at weekends, which had, I now saw, been structured around sport".[19] For many of us, sport serves as a stable point around which to build the rest of our free time. More than this, it provides a sense of continuity, as every week the various sporting stories we are following receive another installment. As Lancaster notes, this can play an important role in taking us outside of the various struggles we may face in the rest of our lives. Sports fandom presents us with a space in which, for the length of the match, we are facing the same struggles as the rest of our fellow supporters and sharing in their joys and sorrows. This not only provides a safe, stable haven from our everyday struggles but also helps us to feel connected with each other.

2.1.3 Fandom brings us together

Like romantic love, sports fandom brings a lot of joy to many. More than this, though, fandom also helps to build and sustain communities.[20] Historian Benedict Anderson famously argued that nations are *imagined communities*. A nation, in his words, "is imagined because the members of even the smallest nation will never know most of their fellow-members, meet them or even hear of them, yet in the mind of each lives the image of their communion".[21] These communities are built in part through shared stories about the past. These may focus on national heroes, military defeats or victories, or the way in which the nation has made an important contribution to the world. In the USA, for example, stories about the founding fathers help to foster a sense of shared national identity. Community-building rituals such as Independence Day, Thanksgiving, and Veterans' Day also play an important role in building this imagined community. These stories and rituals enable a shared sense of community among Americans who have never met one another, who may live thousands of miles away from each other, and who may lead very different lives.

Importantly, calling these communities *imaginary* does not mean that they are not real. The USA is certainly a real country and a real community. The point is that acts of imagination are needed to create these communities. A corporate lawyer in New York and a rural farmer in Utah may never meet each other, and their lives may have very little in common. Stories about the past, a sense of what it means to be an American, and shared rituals all play an important role in helping to build a sense of national community and togetherness. If they succeed, though, then they will have built a real community through these acts of imagination, as they will have created a sense of community and solidarity between these two people.

Sports fan groups can also be viewed as imagined communities.[22] Fan communities are also created through shared stories about the magnificent performances of former heroes and the humbling experience of the catastrophic defeats of the past. Indeed, the historian Mark Dyreson argues that tales of sporting glory and shared struggle form "the backbone of the 'imagined communities' that reside at the core of national cultures".[23] Moreover, Dyreson (2003, 94) claimed that sport should be accepted as "one of the key social technologies for constructing modern nationalism". Sports teams are incredibly effective at fostering a sense of shared national feeling. As the historian Eric Hobsbawm explains:

> What has made sport so uniquely effective a medium for inculcating national feelings, at all events for males, is the ease with which even the least political or public individuals can identify with the nation as symbolized by young persons excelling at what practically every man wants, or at one time in his life has wanted, to be good at. The imagined community of millions seems more real as a team of eleven named people. The individual,

even the one who only cheers, becomes a symbol of his nation himself.[24]

Just as sport can play an important role in developing the imagined communities that are at the heart of national cultures, sports also lead to the development of new imagined communities based on a shared support of sports teams and athletes. Viewed in this way, the athletes serve to represent this wider community. As the author and Arsenal fan Nick Hornby captures it in his autobiographical book *Fever Pitch*, "The players are merely our representatives, chosen by the manager rather than elected by us, but our representatives nonetheless".[25]

The decline of many previously popular forms of community has left people looking for new ways to feel like they are part of a group. Many wealthy countries have seen a decline of large-scale industries such as coal-mining, ship-building, and manufacturing in the last 50 to 60 years. As a result, the communities that existed alongside these industries have also declined and in some cases, almost entirely disappeared. At the same time, other forms of community, such as religious groups and trade unions, have also experienced significant declines in membership.[26] Fan communities help to fill gaps left by these other forms of community in the modern world.[27] As Fowles put it:

> At its core, baseball is a reliable community ritual in a constantly changing, secular world with fewer opportunities for real human connection. As we feel more and more isolated and move further away from our families both physically and mentally, many of us are increasingly looking to spaces like ballparks to bring us together.[28]

Fandom does not only replace traditional forms of community; it can also serve to reinforce them. As Fowles goes on to explain, fandom can help to strengthen family bonds:

> So many baseball devotees I know have shared beautiful stories with me about the relationship between their fathers (or any kind of parental figure, really) and the ballpark. Those with more distant dads talk about the time spent there as special and sacred, the game bridging divides and providing a common love that is otherwise hard to find.[29]

Similarly, literary theorist Mark Edmundson's book *Why Football Matters* begins with how he would spend every Sunday watching football with his father, and ends with how he took his son to play junior football.[30] Watching with his father was an entire ritual, one that Edmundson found deeply meaningful. They would watch, sometimes telling the players what to do, other times just sitting and taking in the game. Sports can form the center of rituals that can bind families and communities together. They can provide a way of helping us feel connected to our families and friends and rooted in the places where we live.[31]

Being a fan can also help people to retain a sense of connection to the places they have left. In our case, following Scottish soccer from the Netherlands helped Alfred to maintain a feeling of being connected to home. When he watches big games in the Premier League and Champions League, Jake will often message his friends in the UK, giving them all something to talk about that isn't just ordinary small talk. This helps him to maintain these friendships, even though it can be hard to keep in touch at such a distance.

When we think of the communities involved in sports fandom, we are likely to first think of partisans, those who root for a particular team. We might think, for example, of how half of Columbus will watch Ohio State take on Michigan, either in bars or at the stadium. We will have more to say about their communities in the next chapter. But it is also important to see that being a fan of a sport rather than a team, being a purist, also has a communal aspect. Mark Edmundson watched football; it didn't necessarily matter which team he watched. We – Jake and Alfred – both watch home soccer from abroad, connecting us to our friends back home. Even though it isn't one of the major sports, there are still legions of soccer fans in the USA. Jake can walk into a bar and chat about soccer to fellow fans, regardless of who they support; or when he goes to the Italian bakery, he'll chat to the owner and his kid about soccer – about Serie A, about the Premier League, and about the video game, FIFA. It doesn't matter who they support, they all just love soccer, and that is what brings them together.

2.1.4 Fandom helps us find an identity

As well as bringing people together, being a fan is often an important part of someone's own identity – it can, in part, make them who they are. This is clear for partisan fans, but we will argue that being a purist, a fan of a sport rather than a team, can also be an important part of someone's identity.

The notion of identity we have in mind might be thought of as one's "social identity" or "ethical identity":[32] how somebody sees themselves, how they live their life in a specific, individualized way, and what makes them the kind of person their friends want to hang out with or the person their spouse loves. Things can be more or less a part of somebody's identity, and these elements can change over time. Bob might say he is a "husband, father, and home-brewer", and each of these elements tells us something about Bob: about how he sees himself and what sort of person he might be.

But no reasonable person imagines that each of these elements plays the same role in determining who Bob is, and if Bob thinks all of these elements are just as important in his life, he has made a serious mistake. Some of these elements might also change over time: Bob became a father at some point, and that changed his identity. But he might also grow tired of home-brewing, so that it fades and becomes an occasional hobby or something he never does, in which case it would no longer be part of his identity. (Though the fact that he used to be a home-brewer may play some small part in making him who he is.) Or to take a sporting example, you might play rugby for a decade only to give it up after too many injuries and having found other things to do with your time: whereas being a rugby player was once part of your identity – it shaped how you lived your life and how other people saw you – it no longer plays that role.

For many fans, being a fan is part of who they are. It means they spend every Sunday from August to February (and the occasional Monday, Thursday, or Saturday) watching the National Football League (NFL); or they spend hours a week watching the Premier League, Champions League, League One, Ligue 1, and the occasional South American derby; or they dress only in replica kits, from the teams they've watched play around the world; or they pay attention to every possible statistic throughout Major League (and perhaps Minor League) Baseball.

In his study of football fandom, sociologist Amir Ben-Porat describes how fandom shapes both the schedule of fans' lives and their relationships with others to such an extent that their football club and fellow fans are among the most important relationships in their life: these relationships define who they are.[33] This can apply to purists, too. Stacey May Fowles describes how her love of baseball became part of her identity:

> Baseball became "my thing", and its stadiums my church, a place to pray in times of hopelessness, the source of a solace I couldn't find elsewhere. I never feel more human, or more sane, than I do inside a ballpark.[34]

By making baseball – and it is baseball, not just a particular team – her "thing", Fowles didn't just enjoy it; she let it shape her life for the better. Another way of putting her point might be that she didn't just feel more human or more sane – she felt as though she was more *herself* when she was in the ballpark.

We can get a deeper understanding of the influence of fandom on identity by returning to the analogy between fandom and love that we discussed in the first chapter. When someone loves another person, this affects their sense of who they are. When someone falls in love with someone else, their sense of who they are changes in response to the interests and identity of the person they love.[35] You may, for example, take on some of your partner's interests, as Jake's wife Hannah did when she became a keen soccer fan.

Fandom shapes people's identities, just like falling in love does. Consider how philosopher Erin Tarver describes becoming a fan of the LSU Tigers:

> As I grew into a fully-fledged fan, I began to care deeply about how "we" did from one season to the next, to understand myself as "a Tiger fan", to feel pride in that status, and to feel resentment for those "fans" whose

devotion, participation, or attention during games did not match mine.[36]

Tarver's increasing fandom involved an increasing sense of identification with the team. The Tigers began to shape her sense of who she was and what her interests were. Similarly, artist Jon Rubin provides a memorable articulation of the importance of fandom for identity in his artwork *You Don't Know Who You Are*.[37] In this work, Rubin produced a scarf for Partick Thistle Football Club. On one side of the scarf are the words "We are Thistle", while on the other side, it reads "You Don't Know Who You Are". Fans, particularly Thistle fans, know who they are, while non-fans do not. This might be a little strong, but it serves to underscore the importance that fandom can have in people's identities.

2.1.5 Being a fan is part of what makes our lives meaningful

As well as shaping *who* we are, being a fan is part of what makes our lives *meaningful*. Take Elias and Dunning:

> Playing and / or watching one sport or another has come to form one of the principal media of collective identification in modern societies and one of the principal sources of meaning in life for many people.[38]

People might just be looking at fandom the wrong way if they're seeing it as *merely* something others spend time on, rather than as something they find worthwhile. We can find support for this claim from research conducted by the psychologists Daniel Wann and Nancy Fast. They found that "sport fandom can and does provide meaning in life". Though the effects of fandom on meaning were modest overall, they were stronger for those fans who identified more closely with their team (i.e. partisans).[39] So, fandom helps give our lives meaning – perhaps not a ton of its meaning, but some of it – and this is stronger when somebody is a fan of a particular team.

But what does it mean for some project to contribute to the meaning of our lives? One plausible way of understanding a meaningful life is, as philosopher Susan Wolf puts it, "active engagement in projects of worth".[40] As Wolf characterizes it, active engagement involves being "gripped, excited, involved".[41] Nobody could possibly doubt that fans – partisans or purists – are gripped, excited, and involved. But this leads to a big question: what is a project of worth, and does fandom involve a project of worth?

It can be easier to see when something is not a project of worth. An adult who has great reading skills but chooses to spend their time reciting the alphabet isn't doing something meaningful, and we shouldn't think he has a meaningful life even if he is deeply gripped by his activity – his hobby is simply not worthwhile enough. Other things can be worthwhile but not important enough to be a source of a meaningful life, such as washing up or going to the dentist.[42] You should do those things, but they won't make your life meaningful. Other things are fun – like drinking or getting high – without being meaningful.

On the other hand, fighting for justice, training to run a marathon (and doing so), or restoring an old farmhouse seem to be worthwhile: they are the sort of projects we see as worth investing time in.[43] Now, there might be debate about which projects are indeed worthwhile. But one important factor in working out whether a project is worthwhile is by looking at whether it is worthwhile *aside from* somebody's enjoyment of that project.[44] Sisyphus, who rolls a boulder up a hill only for it to roll back down, does not have a meaningful life, even if he is deluded into thinking it is meaningful.[45] That is because his task is futile, leading to nothing worthwhile even if he enjoys it. But we can see why it might be worth fighting for justice, running a marathon (and testing the limits of one's own endurance), or restoring a beautiful object – these projects are worth it, aside from our own enjoyment of them.

For many people, being a fan is a part of what makes their lives meaningful. The project of fandom is, to them, a project of worth. But what if they're wrong?

2.1.6 Summary

Before moving on to that question, it's worth summarizing what we've argued so far. We started with the complaint that being a fan is just a waste of time – time that could be spent doing worthwhile things like spending time with a loved one or reading a book. Our response has been that fandom in fact can be deeply beneficial. For one thing, it can make us happy! But it can also allow us to express our emotions while providing a place of stability in times of need. Fandom can bring us together, it can connect us with other fans both near and far, and it can (as both of us are all too aware) provide a link to home when we move far away. Many of us see ourselves as fans; that's to say that fandom shapes our identities, affecting how we spend our time and how we see ourselves. And fandom might even help to make our lives meaningful. After all, we are gripped by our fandom. We had just better hope that fandom is a project of worth …

2.2 ARE BOOK CLUBS ARE BETTER THAN FANDOM?

There are plenty of fun things we can do that shape our identities and give our lives meaning. While some may develop their identity through sports fandom, others may do so by organizing a book club or being a dedicated amateur actor. Maybe there is nothing special about sports fandom in its ability to help people develop an identity and find meaning in their lives. Perhaps other hobbies would do just as well here. Given the problems associated with sport – such as fan violence and racist chants – perhaps it would be better for us to join book clubs or go to the theater instead. We disagree. Watching sports is valuable and is valuable enough to be worthwhile: it can lend meaning to our lives. What's more, watching sports has a *particular* or *distinctive* value.

Sports involve doing things – often very impressive things – with the human body. Philosopher Stephen Mumford argues that "It is pleasing in and of itself to be active".[46] Activity lets us master not just our own bodies but also the world: the swimmer feels comfortable in the water, able to move through it.[47] Mumford tells us about how he learned to dive, which left him feeling "alive, capable, powerful, in control of myself and my surrounds, in direct contact with my world, a human being, embodied".[48] There is surely something to this. We all – outside the skeptical confines of a first-year undergraduate philosophy seminar – recognize there is a world out there, a world we can interact with and test ourselves against. No doubt, we do this in ways other than through playing sports (such as, to use Mumford's other examples of physical skills, playing guitar or performing an operation).[49] But sports provide an arena in which physical skill, rather than end results (nice music or a repaired heart), is the main aim.

There is plenty more to be said in the philosophy of sport about the nature of sports.[50] But that would require another book. We can just stick to the idea that sports are inherently physical and in some sense organized and not simply aimed at conducting some task. Taking part in a rodeo is taking part in sport; catching a bull on the farm is not. Fandom involves appreciating this. We now want to argue that *being a fan* – watching and appreciating what goes on, not participating as an athlete – is worthwhile and is a way of appreciating this value in a distinctive way. It's worthwhile because being a fan can teach us how to live, and being a fan lets us appreciate a certain form of beauty.

2.2.1 The virtues

In reflecting on his childhood watching football with his father, Mark Edmundson tells us: "Through football my father explained the world to me", teaching him about "grace and toughness and manly dignity".[51] We don't need to limit this to one gender: sportspeople, in various disciplines and in various ways, show us dignity in perseverance, struggle, success, and sometimes failure. Stacey May Fowles agrees:

> I am convinced that watching sports makes us better people. What other arena offers both an escape from the trials of life and a place to diligently learn how to live it, a place to both relax and do the necessary work of becoming more human? I certainly know this game has helped me become whole in ways I didn't think possible, made me care about and connect to things outside myself when I was feeling isolated and insular, made me take things as they come rather than agonize about every possible future outcome.[52]

The philosopher Adam Kadlac likewise argues – rightly, we think – that sports can inspire "various forms of moral reflection, sports have the ability to drive spectators' thinking about their own pursuit of the good life".[53] That is to say: by watching sports, we can better understand what it is to live a worthwhile life.

Take the sort of experience we have in reading a novel:

> we might see characters grapple with challenges that we have never faced and think about what we would do in similar circumstances. Or we might see them in a situation that we have been in ourselves, and consider whether they have done better, or worse, than we have. We see character traits on display that we admire and want to cultivate, and traits that we strive to avoid (whether or not we see them in ourselves). We see, in other words, a range of possibilities for how to make our way through the world.[54]

Fandom lets us do the same. From the characteristic ways in which a player deals with an on-pitch challenge (say, a free kick, or a deeply packed defense), to the ways in which their whole careers unfold, Kadlac thinks that watching sports lets us see various ways that people excel (or fail).[55]

One might object that many things allow us to learn more about living the good life. There are two responses here. Firstly, it might be true that watching a play or reading a novel might also educate us about the good life, but few would criticize these pursuits by saying that other areas also allow us to pursue a moral education. And wouldn't somebody have an impoverished view on the world if they took all their lessons from French literature or Shakespeare? These domains shed a different light on various virtues. Although *Wolf Hall* and *American Sniper* might both tell us something about courage, they tell us very different things, and in very different ways, about that virtue. There is value in learning from different sources, and sports give us a different way of learning about how to live our lives. So, the first response here is that sports are one way of learning about how to live our lives.

Secondly, we've seen that sports are valuable *in a specific way*. They are inherently physical and abstracted from the daily grind of work or necessity. Here is how Kadlac puts it, picking up on author David Foster Wallace's reflections on Roger Federer's magisterial skills:[56]

> sports, perhaps more than any other human endeavor, make sense primarily as an exploration of the capabilities and limits of the human body: how fast it can go; how strong it can be; how it can move and manipulate objects in space; how it can coordinate with other bodies to accomplish a shared goal.[57]

As Kadlac admits, other domains of human activity involve the body, but recall that it is primarily in sport that the body's *performance* – rather than, say, how it looks or some product at the end of a process – is central.[58] Sports are the domain of the Olympic motto *Citius, Altius, Fortius*: Faster, Higher, Stronger.

For instance, Foster Wallace wrote about how Federer could glide across the court, how he played with power but also with grace, speed, and an ability to manipulate his opponent. Watching him inspired Foster Wallace who described it in the following way:

> He has, figuratively and literally, re-embodied men's tennis, and for the first time in years the game's future is unpredictable. You should have seen, on the grounds' outside courts, the variegated ballet that was this year's Junior Wimbledon.[59]

No doubt, had Foster Wallace seen the feats that Simone Biles has been able to achieve, he would have been able to write a similar ode praising the way that she has been able to change the field of gymnastics with her sublime talent.

Of course, Federer (like Biles) is a special player, and his skills can inspire us amateurs (and most professionals) only to a certain degree. But the point about this value of fandom isn't just about the specific skills sports stars use; it is about the ways in which they demonstrate to us how we can use our bodies to manipulate the world. They show us something about the limits and abilities of human beings. Stephen Mumford might have learned something about himself when he learned to dive; watching sports allows us to appreciate how we – we human beings – can use our bodies, and also how people can overcome their limits: their pain and suffering, their age and decline. Foster Wallace wrote his piece in 2006, describing a Federer at his peak, in his mid-20s. By 2017, though, Federer was in his mid-30s and had not won a grand slam in five years due to serious injury problems. His ability to come back and win both Wimbledon and the Australian Open is a truly incredible demonstration of mental strength and perseverance that many have found deeply inspiring.

Watching Federer's early success might inspire somebody to alter their squash game or focus their running in a way that emphasizes technique over power; but watching him might also encourage us to persevere, as when we are struggling through a hike and unsure how far our bodies can take us, or when we want to run a distance and just aren't sure if we can. Perhaps looking at how Federer persevered after his setbacks can inspire us to use – and stretch – our own bodies.

Sports can also show us other aspects of the good life beyond physical virtues. To take one final example: Gareth Southgate was best known for missing a vital penalty for England during Euro '96. Later, he was a mediocre manager at Middlesbrough and a competent but unspectacular England under-21s coach. He is now England's most successful manager in over half a century. Not only has he led his team to some very strong tournament finishes (although he has yet failed to win anything), but he has also revived the reputation of the team: for a long while, the reputation of the England team was that they were a bunch of overpaid prima donna individuals, yet now they are known as a tightly-knit, multicultural group who play with pride while speaking up on social issues that afflict their country. Southgate, by any measure, has recovered from his penalty miss and redeemed himself. This took *decades*, including long stints as a nonentity. Looking at his career provokes admiration from many of us, even fans of rival teams. But it can also inspire us, showing us the value of perseverance. This is not *physical* perseverance, like the type Federer showed; rather, Southgate's perseverance is in continuing at his sport, in different ways, despite his failure. This reinforces our point that sports – whether we are witnessing physical or other skills – are a way of seeing the various virtues that exist in life.

2.2.2 Aesthetics

Sports can also offer us immense aesthetic experiences. It is immediately clear from Foster Wallace's discussion of Federer that he isn't just watching somebody do something inspiring; he is watching something *beautiful*. So, too, when we see Simone Biles perform: her blend of grace and power is a sight to behold.

Literary theorist Hans Ulrich Gumbrecht points out that we are sometimes wary of saying that sports have aesthetic qualities; we might be hesitant to admit that calling a skillful move beautiful is doing the same thing as calling a flower beautiful.[60] But he thinks this might just be a form of snobbery.[61] And we think we can make a good case for the idea that sports have their own aesthetic values.[62]

Much as sports might teach us lessons about life, sports have their own aesthetics: an aesthetic grounded in the expression of the human body. Mumford argued that we take pleasure in watching someone exercise physical skills.[63] That is to say nothing of the pleasure that comes along when we witness certain tactics or structure, or the unfolding of a narrative.

But we want to say that there is more than just *pleasure* involved.

One straightforward point to make here is that there are clearly aesthetic qualities in activities like dance. Nobody denies that. And sports are relevantly similar: people do things with their bodies in an organized way, and we value some of those things more than others. In fact, the aesthetic values present in sports are legion: not only are there many sports, each with its own nuances, but there are many ways of successfully – and beautifully – playing each sport. Much as somebody might be enraptured by Gauguin, whereas someone else detests his style and takes pleasure only in Degas, a purist sports fan might appreciate the skilled passing of Barcelona in the late 2000s or the muscularity of Mourinho's Chelsea teams.

Moreover, as the philosopher Andrew Edgar has argued, beauty is not the only aesthetic value to be found in sport.[64] Appreciating a "rigorous defense" or a "begrudging midfield" are also aesthetic experiences that are central to appreciating sport, as are crunching tackles, frenzied clearances, and well-timed interceptions. In Edgar's view, struggle, vulnerability, and the real possibility of failure are more central aesthetic experiences in sport than that of beauty.

We see this in the cricket bowler's effort to get out a stubborn batsman by tempting him into a mistake after bowling a series of similar balls and then switching it up by varying the pace or angle of delivery. We see it in the basketball player's display of power and athleticism in going for the slam-dunk, or the subtler alley-oop that lays the ball off for a team-mate to dunk and which shows off more of the team-based elements of the sport.

While we think that beauty still has some role to play in the aesthetic appreciation of sport, it seems even harder to deny that these other aesthetic experiences are an important part of watching sport.[65] And it is worth adding that these experiences are quite unlike the aesthetic experiences we get in other fields: admiring a rigorous defense is different from admiring a Monet painting or a Beethoven symphony.

It's also worth adding that the aesthetic qualities we see in a team can express something about the place they come from or the values the club holds. In soccer's early years, the British cared about muscularity and individuality, whereas South American football valorized touch, skill, and something closer to dance than war.[66] As well as discussing these nationalistic elements, philosopher John Foster notes that there can be political elements behind sporting styles: socialist team-based play or the struggle of right-wing individualism.[67] No doubt these elements can sometimes be overstated, and there is no meaningful sense in which the USA beating the USSR at ice hockey in 1980 was – despite what some said – a victory for capitalism over socialism. But our sporting preferences can be part of our whole aesthetic outlook. And we might think our sporting preferences can shape our other aesthetic tastes, too. It is surely plausible to think that watching the patient passing style of Pep Guardiola's Barcelona might instill a form of patience that allows viewers to learn to appreciate a work of art that requires more time for contemplation than they were previously willing to allow.

2.3 CONCLUSION

We have argued that being a sports fan is not a waste of time. Rather, it has a positive influence on many people's lives. Being a fan makes many people happy, helps them to deal with their emotions, brings them together with others, and helps people develop their identity and find meaning in their lives. Being a sports fan can also be a way in which people can learn about virtues such as courage and perseverance. Finally, watching sport gives us access to a range of aesthetically valuable experiences.

All of this should not come as a surprise, given that we argued in Chapter 1 that sports fandom is a form of love. Falling in love with someone is also a source of happiness for many (though we can certainly think of relationships that bring more misery than happiness). Falling in love is also a way in which people develop a sense of who they are and helps many people to find meaning in their lives. Viewing sports fandom as a form of love, then, helps us see why fandom has this positive impact on so many people's lives.

This leads us to the final point we want to make about why fandom is not a waste of time and why we have good reason to hold on to fandom even if we could find the same social and personal benefits elsewhere. Fandom is love. Like other forms of love, fandom involves an appreciation of certain qualities (as we argued in Chapter 1). The fans of the Boston Celtics love them for the particular team that they are and the unique identity that they possess. They would not switch to being fans of the LA Lakers if they became more successful – after all, they love the Celtics for *their qualities* and *their successes*, they aren't just trying to support whichever team is most successful at that time. Similarly, someone who loves watching baseball, without loving any team in particular, is a fan of this sport and everything that makes it special.

Part of the defense of being a sports fan, then, should be an acceptance that people simply love watching sports, and that this, like other forms of love, is an attachment to something. A very good reason why sports fans should not seek to get these same benefits elsewhere (through taking part in a book club or watching an opera) is simply that they *love sports* rather than these other activities. Asking sports fans why they do not take up these other activities instead would be like asking someone in a loving relationship why they don't leave their partner for someone else. A perfectly good response for someone to make here is simply that they love their partner, not someone else. Similarly, sports fans can simply reply that they love the club or the sport that they love. This in itself is a reason for them to continue being a sports fan.

Of course, this is not the end of the story. Fandom could still be a bad thing. We'll return to that in depth in the second half of this book. But for now, we can see why people might want to be fans and why – despite allegations to the contrary – they aren't just wasting their time. But what about those partisan fans who love a particular *team*? Well, they face a new raft of objections, and that's what we'll now turn to.

In 1946, Dirk Coffee attended a University of Alabama football game for the first time. After watching them win, Coffee was hooked. Incredibly, after this game, Coffee attended every single game, home and away, that Alabama played until his death in 2013. In total, Coffee attended an astonishing 781 consecutive Alabama games. He was named the best fan in the USA by broadcaster ESPN in 2010.[1] Similarly, Chris Kemp is a fan of the English soccer club Queens Park Rangers (QPR). He attended 1,503 consecutive QPR games between 1989 and 2020. This streak only came to an end when COVID-19 lockdown rules meant that matches had to be played behind closed doors.[2]

It is these fans that might bother people. It is these fans that we might associate with missing your daughter's wedding to watch some stupid match. And it is also partisan fans much more than purists – though perhaps not Coffee and Kemp, who seem a little closer to geeks than evildoers – who we might associate with violence, racist chants, and the complicity with player and club wrongdoing that we'll discuss later.

We think it's clear that there are plenty of good reasons to be a sports fan. But for all we have said in Chapter 2, we might worry that these reasons do not hold for a large swathe of fans – the partisan fans.

In this chapter, we want to focus on two lines of criticism against the partisan. Firstly, the partisan seems to do something

DOI: 10.4324/9781003271277-4

silly. She cares deeply about *her team* — and importantly, she wants her team to win. A purist might not care how the game finishes so long as it is a great game of soccer, basketball or football. But for the partisan, it matters that her team wins. Somebody who thinks watching sport lets us appreciate aesthetic values or moral lessons might think that caring about the result is just *silly*. Some philosophers of sport think that partisans do not *really* believe that the results of sports matches matter. Rather, they are engaging in a form of make-believe. This view is called *fictionalism* by philosophers of sport, as it is the view that partisan fans are engaging in a form of fiction by pretending that the results of sports matches really matter. In this chapter, we will discuss this view and how it can be used as a basis for criticizing partisan fans, or at least those partisan fans who dedicate as much of their lives to fandom as Coffee and Kemp have done. However, we'll argue that fictionalists miss something important about sports fandom: results do matter, at least when fans are part of communities. That's because when the team succeeds, the fan community succeeds.

The second problem is that we might worry that the partisan does badly when it comes to some of the things that we argued, in Chapter 2, make fandom worthwhile. Though the purist can watch and enjoy a game, the partisan is consumed by wanting *her* team to win, and when they fail, she has a terrible time. And so the argument goes, she will often fail, whether they win or lose, to appreciate the aesthetic beauty — or moral lessons — on the pitch, being more invested in success than artistry. Can partisans appreciate the aesthetic elements of sports or learn about the good life? We'll argue that although the partisan's experience of watching sport is different from the purist's, it doesn't have to be seen as inferior.

3.1 PARTISANS INVEST IN THE RESULT[3]

3.1.1 The fictionalist challenge

Let's take on the idea that partisans are doing something silly. They care about the result, and much of their emotional life rests upon, say, whether a ball crosses a line.

Partisan fans can feel awful after a loss, especially after a big one. Greg Miller, a professional counselor and sports fan, saw his San Francisco 49ers lose in the 2013 Superbowl. He was "catatonic". His wife, who had never seen him like this, asked him if he was OK: "And I'm like, no, I don't think I'm OK. I think I'm legitimately hurt and upset by this".[4] He now works to help fans manage their emotions after a loss. These fans can enter moods we might associate with more serious matters: depression and grief. This is something many partisans are familiar with, and we'll share our own stories of feeling awful after a sports match – for days or even weeks – throughout this chapter.

Maybe these fans *are* silly, and it is *wrong* to care about the result in such a way, because it just doesn't matter at all. But a softer, more sophisticated response that has recently gained in prominence in the philosophy of sport is that they are in some sense *pretending* to care. This is called fictionalism. In this section, we'll set out this idea before arguing why results *genuinely* matter for people: because the success of their team is also their own success.

Conveniently for us, one of the proponents of fictionalism is also Alfred's colleague, friend, and fellow Willem II fan, the philosopher Nathan Wildman. He wonders why he can get so emotional when he watches Willem II. He is a loud, passionate fan, elated by a win or heartbroken by a loss; but soon after the final whistle blows, he no longer seems to care. As he puts it: "The outcome no longer matters. Indeed, if you asked, I would say that it never did".[5]

Fictionalists are puzzled by the thought that sports can really, deeply, seem to matter to us, but in other contexts this can fade, and sometimes it can seem as though sports don't *really* matter to us.[6] Now, it seems to us that there are plenty of reasons why sports do indeed matter, and we think that Wildman's experience – where it no longer seems to matter once the final whistle has gone – is a peculiar one. For instance, when Alfred leaves a Willem II game after a loss, he doesn't so easily think that it no longer matters. While a bad result may not ruin his weekend in the way it used to, it certainly requires some getting over. But we don't just want to say that the fictionalists get the starting point wrong; to properly respond to the fictionalist, we need to see what their theory is.

Fictionalists think that partisans are pretending that the results matter. Now, this can sound a bit like it minimizes things, but that isn't quite what the fictionalists are doing. Instead, they think fans are engaging in something like the make-believe involved in watching a film or going to the theater. Obviously, theater is different from sport: there is usually a scripted narrative in theater, sports are competitive, and perhaps most importantly, sports people are *real*. We don't have to imagine that sports stars exist in the way that we might imagine that Romeo and Juliet exist. So, what do fictionalists say sports fans are making believe *about*?[7] They're pretending that the outcome matters.

For instance, the philosopher of sport Steffen Borge claims that "[t]he main fiction present in football … is that winning football matches matters".[8] Wildman says that "the games of make-believe we play when participating in sport involve prescriptions to imagine that the outcome matters".[9] And philosopher Kendall Walton thinks that although fans might (non-fictionally) care about gambling results or the well-being of their team's players, none of this can explain why they are so invested in the result; what explains this is the fiction that it matters.[10]

This view goes some way to explain why partisan fans care when it seems that the result doesn't *really* matter.[11] As Walton puts it: "It's just a story; it's just a game".[12] This justifies why the fan might feel depressed by a result: because in the make-believe, losing really matters. Similarly, it may seem strange for theater audiences to care about the deaths of fictional characters like Romeo and Juliet. The fictionalist can explain why we care here: we care because we are engaging in a form of make-believe in which we pretend that these characters are real. The sports fan and the theater lover are both engaged in a form of make-believe, and this explains why they are able to care so deeply about the result of the match or the lives and deaths of fictional characters. The sports fan is pretending that the result matters just as the theater lover is pretending that these characters really exist.

This view can also do a good job of explaining why fans may have intense emotional reactions while watching the game in the stadium, reactions that quickly fade as soon as they get home. These fans are pretending that the result matters for the duration of the match: when they stop pretending, the emotions related to this pretense disappear. In the same way, theater lovers soon recover from watching Romeo and Juliet die after the lights have gone up and they have left the theater. The theater lover knows these people don't really exist, so once they have stopped pretending that they do exist, they no longer have a reason to care deeply about their fate.

But this still presents a clear problem for the partisan. For one thing, many partisans are often depressed long after the game. But if the fictionalist is right, the emotional tap should shut off once the final whistle goes and the make-believe ends. To care for days or weeks would be like a theatergoer remaining upset about the deaths of Romeo and Juliet for weeks after watching the play. This seems silly. More importantly, many partisans certainly wouldn't claim that they are just *pretending* that the result matters. For many partisans, it *really does matter*. But if the fictionalist is right, then the partisan is deluded: they are so deeply involved in pretending that results matter that they no longer realize that they are pretending.

But the fictionalist position gets it wrong. The fictionalist overstates the ways in which the fan compartmentalizes her fandom and understates the importance of fandom in her broader life — the fictionalist forgets that fans are part of a community.

3.1.2 Why results do matter: partisan communities

As we argued in Chapter 2, sports fandom can bring us together. And — this is the key point that counts against fictionalism — the success of the team *just is* the success of the community. Results matter because they mean that the community succeeds (or fails).

In Chapter 2, we were interested in establishing the idea that fans are somehow part of a community, but this was very general: someone can be part of a community of baseball fans, or a soccer fan in the USA brought together with other fans at 9am on a Saturday in a bar somewhere to watch the Premier League. Now is the time to focus specifically on partisan communities. To do this, we want to look at *two* ways in which sports clubs relate to communities.

Clubs *become* communities, but they also spring up *around* existing communities. We think this is particularly obvious in relation to certain European soccer clubs (what we know the most about), but no doubt it is true elsewhere, too.

For instance, FC Barcelona's *Més que un club* ("more than a club") motto symbolizes their commitment to Catalan nationalism; on the other hand, Real Madrid are part of the Castilian establishment.[13] Journalist Jonathan Wilson, in his fascinating *The Names Heard Long Ago*, tells how SC Hakoah Vienna was formed in 1909 by two Zionists influenced by the idea of Muscular Judaism.[14] By 1925, they became Austrian champions, but they didn't exist just to win competitions: "They existed to promote Zionism and to raise funds for the cause".[15] In Scotland, Glasgow Celtic was formed by an Irish Catholic priest in 1887 to raise money for poor Irish immigrants living in Glasgow. Like many other soccer teams in Germany, Bayer 04 Leverkusen is a team that was formed by workers based at one workplace, in this case the Bayer paint works.

The fact that clubs can be founded with, or become attached to, certain principles and communities explains why you might become a fan of a club. When you are already friends with the workers at Bayer, it makes sense that you'll go along and watch them play, quickly becoming invested in the team because you naturally want to see your friends and colleagues win. If your town has a sports team, if your university is associated with one (or simply has one, as is the case with many major sports in the USA), it's an easy leap from being part of that pre-existing community – a community built around the town, or the job, or the school – to being part of that other community: the community of fans. The same applies to principles: people with similar interests often flock together, so it's no surprise that a Catalan nationalist might also become a Barca fan, because they share the same values.

But sports teams don't just grow *around* existing communities; they also create new communities. As philosopher Erin Tarver puts it, "Sports fandom, far from being inconsequential, is a primary means of creating and reinforcing […] community identities".[16] We mentioned in Chapter 2 how Tarver obsessed over the LSU Tigers, learning about them and wearing the team colors in any way she could.[17] By participating in these rituals, fans are able to feel a closer connection to these communities. Fans hang out together, they cheer for the club, and fans come together as one group.

The sense of community that people find through fandom may be particularly important at times when other forms of community are unavailable. In Chapter 2, we discussed how sports fandom has filled the void left in many people's lives by the decline of other forms of community, such as those associated with religious organizations and large-scale industrial workplaces. Similarly, we have both experienced the special role that fan communities can play for migrants like us. It was through becoming a devoted Willem II fan that Alfred was able to foster a closer sense of connection to the city of Tilburg. By becoming a fan of the Buffalo Bills, Jake has become more connected to the legion of other fans in Rochester and in Western New York more broadly. These are geographical communities, which Jake and Alfred now belong to, and they belong to those local communities partly because they have become part of the fan groups. No doubt many American college students feel the same when they move to a new town: becoming a fan of, say, The Ohio State University can help you feel more part of the community, connected to those around you in Columbus and at Ohio State.

3.1.3 Community success

Why is this relevant to what the fictionalist says, and more broadly, to the idea that results don't really matter? The reason why this is relevant is that it gives us a way of seeing why success actually matters for fans: it matters for them because sporting success is their communal success.

In short, when your team wins, you win. That's because when your team succeeds, your community succeeds. When Arsenal beat Tottenham Hotspur, Arsenal's community of fans win: they get the bragging rights, they support the better team. But this isn't just about bragging rights. Rather, partisan communities are built around *supporting a* team. That means they want the team to win. When the team does win, the community gets what it wanted. In a straightforward way, when the team succeeds, so does the community of fans who want it to win.

We aren't suggesting that the *only* way the community of fans can succeed is when their team wins: the community can succeed when its team loses but plays stylish football. The community might also succeed by doing well *as a community*. Further, being part of the community is itself valuable. As we noted in Chapter 2, the artist John Rubin's Partick Thistle scarf relies on the idea that being a fan helps people know who they are. One side of the scarf tells us that these fans, fans like Alfred, are part of the group that can say "We are Thistle". This is an important part of Alfred's identity and is a part of what makes him who he is. The other side of the scarf reads "You don't know who you are", implying that without this fandom, fans like Alfred would not know who they are. We also argued that fandom can bring meaning to somebody's life. This is bolstered for partisan fans who are part of fan communities. We saw that one hallmark of a life being meaningful is being engaged in projects outside of yourself. One way to do this is through being a member of a community, especially one that is flourishing. Victory is one important way for a community of sport fans to flourish.

You might worry that this means success doesn't really matter; what matters is being part of a community. But that's not the case: what partisans unite around is wanting their team to win. The fact they also benefit from being in a community doesn't take away from that. Wanting their team to win is what *makes them* a community of partisans rather than a community of dog lovers or gourmands.[18] Their team is what brings them together; their team winning gives them what they want. Their team's victory is thus their own victory.[19]

3.1.4 Against the fictionalist

Partisan fan communities are built around wanting a team to win. And when that team wins, the community gets what it wants. It succeeds. So, the fictionalists – along with all those who think that sports results simply don't matter – are wrong. Fans aren't making believe that the result matters. It really does matter. And it matters because being part of a community – where being a member affects the meaningfulness of your life and your very identity – matters. And that community succeeds, and your life goes better, when your team wins.

There are limits to our argument. For one, some fans might not be part of any community – they may watch alone at home. Our argument covers the fans who watch in the stadium, and it covers all those who have a connection to other fans: who watch together, who chat about the game, who see themselves as part of that community. Yet, an even simpler argument might apply to loner fans: these fans adopt a sort of project of being fans of a club. That project succeeds when their club wins. So, they succeed when their club wins. This argument might be simpler, but we do think that fans who are in a community get more out of their fandom and that this was worth explaining in more depth.

We also think the fictionalist has some insights: when someone is trying to become a fan, they may well need to make believe that the result matters. But, after a while they'll stop pretending – the result will really matter. Fans might also sometimes tell themselves that the result doesn't matter, that it's all a game of make-believe, in order to get over the pain of a hard loss. But this also tells us something about how the fictionalist goes wrong. Next time your team loses, try to think it was just a game of make-believe, and the result didn't matter: if you are like us, then there's a good chance that this won't work, and the pain of defeat will remain. We think it's perfectly reasonable to be sad about losing an important match, and this sadness might go on for a little while – and it might even be hard to overcome. Still, there are limits to how long this should last. Someone might have a meaningful job, but it's a problem if that job means they never have time to enjoy the other things that make their life worth living. Likewise, if your love for your team means you are a wreck for a month every time they lose in the play-offs, if it stops you having a career, if it ruins your relationships, then fandom can certainly be a bad thing. We've argued that feeling sad about a result is reasonable; what's silly is when this emotion takes over your life.

3.2 PARTISANS CAN'T REALLY APPRECIATE SPORTS

3.2.1 Advantages of watching sport as a purist

But here's another problem. Perhaps it's fine to care about the result, but does that stop you from appreciating many of the things that make watching sports valuable: does it stop you from seeing sporting beauty, from learning about how to be a good person? Perhaps being a partisan gets in the way of many of the things that, we argued in Chapter 2, make sport worthwhile. To understand this view, let's think about how partisanship can prevent us from appreciating sporting excellence.

Things were finely poised in the 52nd minute of a crucial group match between Scotland and the Czech Republic in the 2020 UEFA European Football (Soccer) Championship. An evenly balanced first half had ended with the Czech Republic taking the lead before half-time. Scotland began the second half confidently and were looking to convert their pressure into an equalizing goal. A Scotland shot from distance was blocked by the Czech defense, and the ball ran into the path of Czech striker Patrick Schick on the halfway line. Schick took a quick look up, saw that the Scottish goalkeeper David Marshall was off his line, and unleashed a perfectly weighted lobbed shot from 54 yards out that sailed over the helpless Marshall's head and into the net.

Schick's goal not only showed impressive quick-thinking and remarkable athletic technique; it was also a goal of great beauty, for which Schick was awarded the goal of the tournament. Unfortunately, as a committed Scotland supporter, Alfred could appreciate none of these things. Rather than seeing an expertly executed piece of outrageously skillful improvisation, Alfred saw only defensive errors and poor positioning. Rather than admiring the best goal of the tournament, Alfred experienced only despair that Scotland's first appearance at the Euros in 24 years already seemed destined to end in an early exit.

Alfred's inability to appreciate this majestic goal points us towards a general problem. Partisan fans watch the game in a competitive way.[20] Watching a game in this way involves watching it with one aim in mind, namely seeing your team triumph. The key moments of the match are not appreciated for the beauty of the move, or the high levels of sporting talent being displayed, at least not primarily. Instead, the focus is on the impact of these moments on the team's chances of winning. This is why Alfred responded to Schick's beautiful goal with disappointment and despair rather than admiration or joy. Purists, on the other hand, watch sport in order to appreciate the sporting talents and athletic beauty being displayed. They are able to admire every sporting achievement being displayed, regardless of its impact on the result.

As we saw earlier, love affects what we pay attention to. Partisans will focus on their own team's performances, achievements, and failures and pay far less attention to those of the opposition. While partisans may be able to provide in-depth individual evaluations for each member of their team, they are likely to have a much more superficial impression of how the opposition played. When Alfred saw Schick's goal, he wasn't even aware which Czech player had scored. He knew instantly, though, that Scotland's David Marshall and Jack Hendry were culpable.

The competitive and one-sided ways in which partisans watch sport may seem to be reasons to avoid being a partisan. The philosopher Stephen Mumford makes this kind of argument.[21] He has some expertise in the matter, having once been a committed partisan fan of Sheffield United Football Club who became purist. He argues that purists are able to appreciate much more of what goes on in sports matches than partisans are. The purist will be able to appreciate the athletic talents, beautiful moves, and clever tactical approaches of either side, while the partisan will only appreciate their own team's merits – and will be overly critical of, or defensive about, their own team's flaws. While the partisan's attention will be on their team and their chances of winning, the purist can focus on truly understanding the sporting contest taking place in front of them. The purist would be able to appreciate that Schick's goal involves both incredible skill *and* defensive mistakes; the partisan Scotland fan would struggle to see beyond their sporting despair to recognize the talent and the beauty of Schlick's play.

We agree that partisans and purists watch sport differently. However, we think that both ways of watching sport are valuable. While these different ways of watching sport may provide quite different kinds of experiences to spectators, they may nevertheless be equally valuable ways of appreciating sport.[22] In order to make this case, let's start by considering another Scotland soccer match that took place seven months before the game against the Czech Republic.

3.2.2 In defense of watching as a partisan

Scotland were aiming to qualify for their first major tournament in over 20 years. To do so, they needed to beat Serbia in a one-off match in Belgrade, the Serbian capital. A fantastic piece of close control from Ryan Christie followed by a perfectly placed shot off the post and into the goal had given Scotland the lead in the second half. Having missed several chances to further their lead, Scotland started defending deeply, and Serbia piled on the pressure. As the match moved towards injury time, it looked like Scotland had done just enough to secure a famous victory. But in the last minute of normal time, a Serbian corner found an unmarked Luka Jović, whose downward header bounced off the ground and into the net past the despairing dive of goalkeeper David Marshall, taking the game to extra-time. The Scotland players were visibly dejected, and it took an outstanding save from Marshall to deny Serbia a winning goal.

With the match finishing 1–1, the game went to penalties, and those with a long history of supporting Scotland prepared themselves for another heroic failure. After four well-taken penalty kicks from each side, the shoot-out was tied at 4–4, and each team had one last penalty to take. Scotland's Kenny McLean sent the goalkeeper the wrong way to make it 5–4 to Scotland, meaning that Serbia needed to score their final penalty to stay in the match. As Serbia's Aleksandar Mitrović walked purposefully up to take the kick, the referee explained to Scotland goalkeeper Marshall that if the penalty were saved, it might have to be checked by the video referee. Scotland fans waited for the high-scoring Mitrović to do what seemed to be inevitable and take the score to 5–5. But instead, Mitrović shot into the bottom right corner of the goal, and Marshall dived superbly to keep it out. As the rest of the Scotland team rushed to celebrate, goalkeeper Marshall spent an agonizing five seconds checking with the referee that his save would count and that Scotland had indeed won the match. The referee confirmed this just as Marshall's team-mates arrived to celebrate with him.

While this moment would have been dramatic to any watching soccer fan, we think that only partisans would be able to fully experience the drama of this moment. For Scotland fans, Marshall's agonizing wait was also *their* agonizing wait. Other soccer fans may have been able to sympathize with Marshall's experience and feel some vicarious relief when the referee confirmed that Scotland had won. But Scotland fans did not feel relief for someone else; they felt relief for *themselves*. They did not feel vicarious joy for the Scotland team; the fans' delight was a direct response to the fact that their team had qualified.

The philosopher Ray Elliott has argued that only those who are invested in the outcome of a sports match in the way that partisans are will be capable of experiencing the drama of the match. While purists may experience an attack as "likely to succeed", the partisan will "feel its menace, since it is his team's goal that is threatened". While the purist will watch the attack break down, the partisan "will feel a sense of deliverance".[23] Only partisans, then, will be able to properly experience the full dramatic potential of watching sport.

It seems, then, that both partisans and purists are able to appreciate something important in sport that the other cannot. Only partisans will be able to fully experience the drama of a sports match. But only purists will be able to experience all of the beauty, talent, and expert decision-making on display. So, where does this leave the sports fan? Should they choose to watch sport in a way that allows them to appreciate the beauty and talent on display? Or, should they instead opt for partisanship and fully immerse themselves in the drama of the game?

3.2.3 Different forms of fandom are OK

Thankfully, there is no need for sports fans to make such a stark choice. Fans can engage with different sports matches in different ways. A committed, partisan Buffalo Bills fan can enjoy a National Football League game between the Arizona Cardinals and the Green Bay Packers as a purist. The same fan may engage with other sports like basketball purely from the position of a purist, or be a fan of the National Women Soccer League's OL Reign, but watch major league soccer as a purist. Indeed, some sports may not lend themselves to partisan attachments and may encourage spectators to be purists. Although golf fans might have favorite players, these players will eventually retire (whereas many team sports clubs have been around, and will continue, for centuries). For this reason, it makes sense to enjoy golf and not be solely focused on the success of one player.

We should also note that partisans and purists, as we have sketched them, occupy the two extreme ends of those forms of fandom. We said in Chapter 1 that there are extreme partisans and more moderate ones. Here, we've been presenting this objection in terms of the extreme partisan: in terms of somebody who just wants to see her side win.

Most sports fans will be less extreme and will be able to combine elements of partisanship and purism in the way they watch sport.[24] A committed, partisan fan of Buffalo Bills may nevertheless be able to appreciate some of the talent and athletic beauty displayed by the opposition. Such a fan may also reject a win-at-all-costs attitude and want the Bills to win but to do so by playing the right way and by obeying the rules. Some fans manage to achieve this even when facing their most fierce rivals. The rivalry between Barcelona and Real Madrid is one of the most famous and fierce rivalries in world soccer. Yet when Ronaldinho starred in a 3–0 win for Barcelona over Madrid in 2005, a section of the Madrid fans gave him a standing ovation for his wonderful second goal. This shows that it is possible to be a passionate partisan and still be capable of appreciating talent from the opposition.[25] Perhaps the best option, then, would be to choose a position that involves a clear allegiance to a team with an ability to appreciate the sporting virtues and beauty of both sides.[26]

The question remains, though, of how to achieve this in practice. It is all very well to say that partisans should try to appreciate the qualities of the opposition, but this can be difficult to achieve in the heat of an important match. Not many

Scotland fans would have been able to appreciate the beauty and talent of Schick's goal as they watched their Euro 2020 dreams crumble in front of their eyes. How can a committed partisan appreciate the sporting achievements that damage the team they love?

One suggestion is that fans can switch between the partisan and purist ways of watching sport.[27] At different times, a fan might be watching in the competitive mode of a partisan, while at others, she is watching in the mode of the purist and is seeking to appreciate the talent and beauty of the match. This may be something that happens while a match is being played. A partisan may spend most of the match watching in a competitive way but find herself lost in the beauty of a particular passage of play from the opposition.

What seems more common, though, is that the purists' way of watching the game can be entered into later. Scotland fans, like Alfred, were perfectly capable of appreciating the beauty and technique of Schick's goal after the match had ended. While some may have needed a day or two to grieve for the damage done to Scotland's Euro 2020 hopes, eventually most Scotland fans were able to appreciate the beauty of this wonderful goal and Schick's amazing technique. When we watch the key moments of a match again, knowing that the result is already determined, even committed partisans are often able to switch to a more purist appreciation of the game.[28] By switching between these two perspectives, fans may be able to experience the full drama of a sporting contest while also being able to appreciate the talents and beautiful play from both sides.

It's also worth noticing that partisans don't want sheer success in some absurd, adding-up-wins-is-all-that-matters way. Instead, the partisan wants her side to *be the best*. But this means that the partisan needs to appreciate what it means to be the best.[29] To take a non-sporting example, you might want your friend to win an art competition, but you don't want them to win through nepotism or bribery. You want them to create the best artwork. To understand what the best artwork is, you need to appreciate *artistic beauty*. And you might see that although your friend's work was great, someone else produced a real masterpiece. That's compatible with being upset that your friend lost.

In the 2022 Divisional Round game, Jake's team, the Buffalo Bills, went to Arrowhead Stadium to take on the Kansas City Chiefs. They lost in a heart-breaking overtime period. But the game was fantastic, with 25 points being scored and the lead changing hands several times just in the last 2 minutes. It was a painful loss, but it was *obviously* a brilliant game: Jake could appreciate the sheer sporting quality of the contest between two great teams, and he remarked on it during the game. One might say that he became a purist for a minute – but why not just say he could appreciate how good Patrick Mahomes and the Chiefs were? Of course, he didn't enjoy it in the way a purist would (the sheer pain of loss outweighed much of his appreciation of the game), but that certainly doesn't mean he couldn't appreciate the sporting excellence on display.

Perhaps it is easier for him, being a newer fan of the Bills. That seems a cheap shot: philosopher Adam Kadlac, a lifelong Wisconsin fan, recalls a game when he was deeply committed to his team winning, and he was "disappointed at the outcome" but remembers "consciously thinking at numerous points what a good game it was".[30] And we (or our critics) would be giving ourselves far too much credit if we were to say that only philosophers of sport can appreciate the good play of rivals! In the UK, fans of ice-hockey often applaud the other team, and booing the other team is unacceptable – so even if some fans in some sports are antagonistic to others, we have no reason to think this is some essential feature of sport fandom.[31] Perhaps the important lesson is that even extreme partisans don't simply want victory; they want to be the best – and to be able to recognize they are the best, they need to appreciate good football, or soccer, or baseball, whichever team is demonstrating it.

Being a partisan certainly clouds some of our appreciation of sporting values, but perhaps we don't need to choose between being a partisan and appreciating sporting beauty. So, even if the partisan misses out on something, they also get other joys, and we need to be careful not to overstate just how much the partisan might miss out on by, for example, claiming that they will be completely unable to appreciate sporting beauty from the opposition.

It is also worth noting that the sporting world would be significantly diminished if it were to lose either the partisan or the purist. We need impartial voices to judge whether one team is better than another, whether it was a lucky victory, and to help us appreciate some of the sheer beauty at play in sport. But think how diminished the sporting landscape would be without the passionate supporters of particular clubs! Some of the most exciting sporting contests have more to do with the rivalries between the two groups of fans than with the two groups of players.[32] The Old Firm derby between Glasgow Celtic and Glasgow Rangers is one of the most famous soccer rivalries in the world. It is broadcast around the world, including in countries like the Netherlands where no other Scottish games are shown. The interest in this match, though, comes from the fierce rivalry between the two sets of fans, which creates a notoriously hostile atmosphere for the away team and often results in fiercely competitive and aggressive matches. Without these fiercely partisan fans, this match would be of little interest to anyone outside Scotland.

The COVID-19 pandemic provided clear evidence of just how important partisan fans are to sport. As many European soccer matches had to be played without an audience, players, journalists, and those watching on TV all complained that the matches were not the same without supporters. This even led some clubs to play recordings of their fans singing while matches were being played. Importantly, it was the partisan fans in particular that were being missed, not the absence of spectators in general. Without the cheering for the goals, the booing of the opposition, and the protests at controversial refereeing decisions, the matches were nowhere near as exciting. Without partisans, the sports world would be a far poorer place.[33]

3.3 CONCLUSION

We have defended partisan sports fans against two related objections. First is the idea that partisan fans are those who are so deeply involved in making believe that results of sports matches matter that they can no longer recognize the pretense. Against this, we argued that for at least some partisan fans, the results of sports matches really do matter, as this is what constitutes success for their fan communities. It is perfectly reasonable, then, for these sports fans to remain emotionally involved in the outcome of the match long after it has ended. These results matter to these communities, and these communities matter to these fans.

We also responded to the objection that partisan fans cannot fully appreciate sports matches. While it may be true that being a partisan can act as an obstacle to certain forms of appreciation, it also enables fans to fully take in the dramatic qualities of matches. Alfred might have missed out on something when he watched Scotland lose to the Czech Republic. But he also benefits plenty when his Scotland side wins. He is unfortunate in being a fan of Scotland, a team that doesn't win in all that much, but perhaps that heightens the sensation of victory when it eventually arrives. When they win, he wins; and when they win, he gets a thrill that purists miss out on.

He can also – except when he's really wrapped up in things – appreciate the other side doing well. After all, partisans don't need to be driven solely by racking up as many wins as possible; instead, many of them want their team to excel. To want that, and appreciate it, means that the partisan will often be able to appreciate, albeit begrudgingly, when the other side has played well. So, these aesthetic values will often still be in reach for the partisan, and by a similar form of argument, we can see that the partisan will be able to learn some moral lessons from what happens on pitch, too.

This, though, is far from the only criticism made of partisans. This form of fandom is also criticized for encouraging an adversarial mentality, a mentality that can lead fans into grave moral wrongdoing. In the next two chapters, we will consider this form of criticism.

In 1969, tensions were running high between neighboring Central American countries El Salvador and Honduras. Honduras is a much larger country, with a landmass five times bigger than El Salvador's. However, El Salvador had a much bigger population, with 3.7 million people compared with Honduras's 2.6 million. El Salvador's large population, combined with the fact that much of the land was owned by a wealthy landowning elite, left little land for poorer Salvadoran farmers. This led many Salvadorans to migrate to largely uninhabited areas of Honduras to settle and start farming. In 1967, the Honduran government responded by passing a land reform law that declared that the land occupied by these Salvadoran migrants could be seized and given to native Hondurans. The government also started seizing land from native Salvadorans who had legal ownership of their land in Honduras. This quickly led to nearly 300,000 Salvadorans becoming refugees and being forced from their homes and the land they had cultivated.[1]

At the height of these tensions, the two countries faced each other in a three-legged tie to determine which of them would qualify for the 1970 World Cup. The first game was played in Honduras on June 8th. The night before the match, Honduras fans created a loud disruption outside the hotel where the El Salvador players were sleeping, hoping that this would

DOI: 10.4324/9781003271277-5

make them play badly the next day. The Honduran team won 1–0, scoring their goal in the final minute of the match. The next game was played a week later in El Salvador. The night before the game, the Salvadoran fans smashed the windows of the hotel where the Honduran players were staying "and threw rotten eggs, dead rats, and stinking rags inside".[2] The Honduran flag was burned in the stadium before the game. During the national anthems, a dirty dishrag was raised on the flagpole in its place. The Salvadorans won 3–0, setting up a third game in a neutral venue. After the match, Salvadorans started rioting and attacking traffic heading to Honduras. Two Honduran fans died as a result.[3] When news of these attacks reached Honduras, Hondurans responded by attacking Salvadoran migrants, forcing them from their homes, beating and robbing them, and forcing them back to El Salvador.[4] The Salvadoran government accused the Hondurans of committing genocide and asked the Organization of American States to intervene, a request that was denied.

The final match took place in Mexico City on June 26th. El Salvador won an exciting match 3–2. Violence again followed. On the day of the match, the Salvadoran government broke off diplomatic relations with the Hondurans in response to the lack of punishment for those who had attacked Salvadoran migrants. Just over two weeks later, on July 14th, the two countries were at war, and the Salvadoran air force was attacking targets in Honduras. Four days later, the two governments agreed to a cease-fire. This war later became known as The Football War or The Soccer War.[5]

Incredibly, this is not soccer's only war. On May 13th, 1990, a league match in the former country of Yugoslavia between Dinamo Zagreb (Croatia) and Red Star Belgrade (Serbia) became known as "the football match that started a war".[6]

Political tensions were running high before the match, as the previous week's Croatian elections had been won by the pro-independence candidate Franjo Tudjman. Croatian independence was fiercely opposed by the Serbian leader Slobodan Milošević, who started a propaganda campaign claiming that Serbs in Croatia were facing genocide. The fans of both teams used the match as an opportunity to give voice to their fierce political opposition to each other. The Serbian Red Star fans chanted "Zagreb is Serbian" and "We'll kill Tudjman", while the Dinamo fans pelted them with stones.[7] The Red Star fans then began to destroy the stadium and to throw seats at the Dinamo supporters. The violence eventually spilled onto the pitch. While the Red Star players quickly left, several Dinamo players stayed, leading to the moment that would turn Dinamo captain Zvonimir Boban into a Croatian national hero. When Boban witnessed a police officer attacking a Dinamo fan, he ran towards the officer and jumped up and kneed him in the face. Eventually, the police managed to bring the riot under control. This riot, though, became known as the unofficial start of the Croatian War of Independence. The Dinamo fans have even built a monument outside the stadium with an inscription that reads: "To all the Dinamo fans for whom the war started on May 13, 1990, and ended with them laying down their lives on the altar of the Croatian homeland".[8]

4.1 WAR MINUS THE SHOOTING

It would clearly be an exaggeration to say that either of these matches led to wars that would not have happened otherwise. In both cases, the political tensions existed long before the matches took place and arose from complex political issues rather than simply football rivalries. However, the idea that sports matches can heighten existing intergroup tensions has a long history. In 1945, shortly after the end of the Second World War, the Soviet Union team FC Dynamo Moscow toured the UK, playing a series of matches against local teams. The aim was to further develop positive relations between the UK and the USSR after their successful allied victory in the war. But the English writer George Orwell (author of *Animal Farm* and *1984*) claimed that it had the opposite result and served "to create fresh animosity on both sides".[9] This, Orwell claimed, should be no surprise, as it is in the nature of international sports contests that they "lead to orgies of hatred".[10]

Orwell was not opposed to sport in general. Games between friends and neighbors played for enjoyment and exercise are fine. He had no problem with, say, a session of pick-up basketball or a lunchtime game of tennis. The problem comes "as soon as the question of prestige arises, as soon as you feel that you and some larger unit will be disgraced if you lose". When this is the case, "the most savage competitive instincts are aroused". This leads to a situation where the sporting contest becomes "bound up with hatred, jealousy, boastfulness, disregard of all rules and sadistic pleasure in witnessing violence: in other words it is *war minus the shooting*".[11]

The problem, according to Orwell, is not how the players behave. Rather, it is the people watching, "who work themselves into furies over these absurd contests, and seriously believe – at any rate for short periods – that running, jumping and kicking a ball are tests of national virtue". These contests encourage nationalism among the fans, which Orwell describes as "the lunatic modern habit of identifying oneself with large power units and seeing everything in terms of competitive prestige". While Orwell did not claim that sports matches create international rivalry, he did think that they, "make things worse by sending forth a team of eleven men, labeled as national champions, to do battle against some rival team, and allowing it to be felt on all sides that whichever nation is defeated will 'lose face'".[12] Partisan sports fandom – where we succeed when the team succeeds, as we argued in Chapter 3 – makes existing national rivalries worse.

The Swedish philosopher of sport Torbjörn Tännsjö takes this idea one step further, claiming that sporting and political national rivalries "reinforce each other".[13] This certainly seems plausible when we think of the El Salvador vs. Honduras and Dinamo Zagreb vs. Red Star Belgrade matches. The atmosphere at these matches was so hostile because of the ongoing political tensions between the rival groups. These matches, then, made these existing political tensions even worse.

It is not only international sporting contests that might be worryingly adversarial. In March 2022, Querétaro hosted Atlas in Mexico's Liga MX. The match was stopped by fan violence – blamed on a section of Querétaro's fans, the barras bravas (fierce gangs). Horrific videos circulated showing Querétaro fans beating and kicking limp, seemingly lifeless bodies. Fans used chairs, knives, belts, and other objects to assault one another. Reports varied as to how many people were injured, from nine hospitalized and two in critical condition, to over 50 hospitalized and several in critical condition.[14] Other reports questioned the official statistics and claimed that people certainly died.[15] But these numbers do not quite capture the sheer violence involved, seen by many in videos that circulated on Twitter. It was horrifying. A father, sheltering his child, was attacked; pictures showed a family, with two young kids, fleeing across the pitch.

We have, then, a general objection to partisan fandom: that this fandom encourages vicious adversarial acts and attitudes. Fairly obviously, this can lead to violence, and the moral problems with that are clear. In Chapter 5, we'll consider how fans should respond when their fellow fans are violent. But first, we want to consider a problem that concerns the very nature of being a partisan, and that is the problem of *adversarialism*.

Passionately wanting one team to win a sporting contest can easily lead us morally astray by encouraging a strong form of animosity towards those outside of one's community. As philosopher Randolph Feezell argues, strongly identifying with a team in a sporting contest and hoping desperately that they win is likely to lead to bad attitudes like hatred or resentment towards those who may stand in the way, such as the opposing team or the match officials.[16] This is even more likely to happen when there is a pre-existing rivalry between the two groups and especially if the sporting rivalry overlaps with a political rivalry. One reason why these bad attitudes should be avoided is that they may lead us to harm others by acting violently or offensively towards them. We will see in Chapter 5 how some groups of fans, like violent hooligans, band together seemingly just to fight rivals. But a hateful attitude may also be bad for its own sake, even when it does not lead people to harm others. Why should a supporter of the Dallas Cowboys feel intense hatred towards a group of strangers cheering on the Washington Commanders? Isn't there something quite ridiculous about feeling hatred for people you have never met simply because they support a different team from the one that you support? If sports fandom gives rise to this hatred, then wouldn't we better to avoid becoming a partisan fan altogether?

A related problem with this form of adversarialism is that it may lead to the celebration of one's own group at the expense of the individual. Partisans celebrate their club, their team, the colors, and the badge. They celebrate the Green Bay Packers or the Indiana Fever. To the extent that individual players are celebrated by partisan fans of teams, it is mainly as representatives of this group identity. As Torbjörn Tännsjö has argued, the celebration of group identities like this can come at the expense of the individuals involved.[17] Players and coaches are viewed as expendable. As soon as fans decide that they are no longer useful to the team, they call for them to be sacked or transferred. For example, Arsène Wenger was a hugely successful manager of Arsenal Football (soccer) Club. He was the first foreign manager to win the English Premier League and FA Cup double, in 1998. In 2004, his Arsenal team not only won the league but also went the entire league season without being beaten, something managed only once before by an English team. By 2013, though, Arsenal had gone six years without winning a trophy, and a growing number of fans demanded that he be sacked. This discontent grew into a movement that combined the unpleasant and the bizarre. Wenger was subject to widespread hate and abuse, and placards reading "Wenger Out" began appearing in increasingly strange places, including Wrestlemania, an international match between Fiji and New Zealand, a London protest against Donald Trump, a Coldplay concert in Singapore, and a rugby sevens match in Vancouver. Wenger was reported to have been left "shell shocked" by the "very close, personal, and nasty" abuse that he received after a 1–1 draw with Crystal Palace in 2016.[18] This treatment of a man widely viewed as the greatest ever Arsenal manager highlights how partisans can become so fixated on the success of the group that they end up mistreating individuals.[19]

If being a partisan fan can lead to hatred, rioting, hooliganism, and abusing our team's heroes, doesn't that show that it is not OK to be this kind of fan? Perhaps unsurprisingly, we think the truth is a bit more complicated.

4.2 CHARITY AND KINDNESS

During Scotland's first lockdown of the COVID-19 pandemic in March 2020, the soccer season was brought to a premature end. Suddenly players, coaches, and matchday staff found themselves with little to do. In response to this, Alfred's favorite Scottish team, Partick Thistle Football Club, decided to temporarily change its name to Partick Thistle *Family* Club. With most Scots having to maintain strict social distance from other households, the club pledged "to do everything it can to look after its full family of supporters and make sure no fan feels isolated in the tough times ahead".[20] The club was true to its word. Players and coaching staff began phoning the club's fans to chat with them and to help them deal with isolation.[21] The club's charitable trust delivered 9,000 free meals to vulnerable local people as part of its COVID-19 response program.[22] The club's fans were also quick to help and raised thousands of pounds for a local healthcare charity to help fund virtual visits for isolated COVID-19 patients and rest and recuperation stations for frontline staff.[23] Thistle was far from the only club to respond to the pandemic in this way.

Other times, the fans themselves make the charitable moves. Buffalo Bills fans pride themselves on their generosity. This was repaid after they lost to the Kansas City Chiefs in the 2022 Play-offs. As we mentioned in Chapter 3, this was a fantastic game – even though it was heartbreaking for Jake. The Bills were in the lead with 13 seconds left, only for the Chiefs to tie the game and win in overtime. Chiefs fan Brett Fitzgerald suggested that fans pay tribute to Josh Allen, the losing quarterback, by each donating $13 to his foundation, benefiting the Oishei Children's Hospital of Buffalo. This raised over $300,000.[24]

While it is true that partisan fandom can lead fans to be adversarial and celebrating their group at the expense of others, being a committed fan of a sports team can also lead people to help others. Partisan fandom can encourage both good and bad behavior. Sports fandom is in good company here. Religious belief has inspired many acts of charity, compassion, and solidarity. It has also led to hatred, warfare, and sectarian violence. Love and friendship can bring out the best in people. But they can also inspire jealousy, cronyism, and favoritism. The fact that love and friendship can inspire bad behavior should not lead us to think that love and friendship are best avoided altogether.

Moreover, the cases of sports matches leading to extremes of violent behavior are exceptional. The matches El Salvador vs Honduras and Dinamo Zagreb vs Red Star Belgrade only led to violence because of the background political situations. Perhaps it is a bad idea to hold sports matches between two fiercely opposed groups on the brink of war. But this does not show that sports matches in general are to be avoided. It is also a bad idea to invite two people who have recently undergone a bitter divorce to the same dinner party. But this is not a reason to avoid dinner parties altogether![25]

Similarly, while it is true that sports fans can celebrate the group at the expense of the individual, it is simply not true to say that this is generally the case. In fact, it seems more common for fans of particular teams to also become attached to the individuals playing for that team – though, as we will see in Chapter 6, this can itself have downsides. Fans of smaller teams enjoy seeing former players go on to achieve great things at a higher level. Alfred and many other fans of Partick

Thistle took great pleasure in the team's former center-back Jack Hendry competing in the Champions League for Club Brugge, especially when they secured a draw against a Paris Saint Germaine team featuring Lionel Messi.

Fans are also quick to come to the help of former players in times of need. Fans of English soccer club Blackburn Rovers raised over £20,000 to help pay for the costs of a care home for their former player Tony Parkes, who had dementia.[26] The tragic death of Kobe Bryant in a helicopter crash in 2020 led to an outpouring of grief from fans of LA Lakers fans and basketball more generally. The genuine grief that sports fans feel when a favorite player dies makes it clear that the celebration of group identities does not have to come at the expense of appreciating the value of individuals.

4.3 LOYALTY

While it is true that being a partisan can lead people to be adversarial, it can also promote acts of kindness and foster genuine bonds of affection between fans and players. Being a committed fan can lead to good as well as bad behavior, making it tempting to conclude that fandom is neither good nor bad but simply neutral. There is, though, more to say here.

Fandom can not only inspire occasional acts of kindness but can also be a means through which people develop and display the virtue of loyalty. Those who stick with their team through thick and thin – through both victory and defeat, promotion and relegation, play-off successes or losing seasons – display the virtue of loyalty. Consider the case of Manchester City fans. In the 1998–99 season, City were in the third level of English soccer (then called Division Two) for the first time in their history. Expected to immediately win promotion, the club had a disappointing start to the season. A defeat to

York City left them 12th in the table, ten places away from an automatic promotion place. Remarkably, though, the support from the club's fans remained strong throughout this period. The club's average attendance for the season was 28,261, an extremely high figure for the English third tier – more than twice their nearest league rival's attendance.[27] As City's then manager Joe Royle recalls, the City fans "broke records everywhere we went [...] their support for the club through thin and thin has been outstanding".[28] After a long and difficult season, the fans' loyalty was eventually rewarded when the team came back from 2–0 down to win the play-off final and secure promotion.

The philosopher Nicholas Dixon argues that this kind of devotion is a form of loyalty.[29] Loyalty is the admirable virtue of sticking with one's relationships and group attachments.[30] We can see why the City fans' devotion can be seen as a form of loyalty by comparing their behavior with that of a loyal friend. When times are tough, a loyal friend will stick by you and help you through the bad times. When you've just been dumped, a loyal friend will be there to give you a shoulder to cry on and maybe even a room to sleep in. When you've failed to land your dream job, a loyal friend will be there to help you find some perspective or to help you think through how you can be more successful next time. On the other hand, a disloyal friend, if such a person can be called a friend, will abandon you as soon as times get hard. They will be there for you when you are celebrating a promotion but will mysteriously disappear when you get made redundant. They will be there for your wedding but will be too busy to give you sympathy during your divorce. Loyalty to a friend strikes us as morally admirable. We think it is good that people are able to stick by their friends through thick and thin and generally bad when people abandon friends who are going through difficult times.

The Manchester City fans who stuck by their team at their lowest moments demonstrate a similarly admirable form of commitment to their club. When their club hit their lowest moments, these fans were still there giving their support. Similarly, fans of NBA team the Sacramento Kings have had 16 consecutive losing seasons, the most ever in the history of the NBA. Yet these fans continue to turn up to support their team and to encourage them on to that elusive victory. Just as we should admire those who stand by their friends and romantic partners when times are tough, so too should we admire those who stick by struggling sports teams.[31]

These fans not only *show* loyalty; they may also be *developing* the virtue of loyalty in themselves. According to the Ancient Greek philosopher Aristotle, we learn to become virtuous people by performing virtuous actions and developing the habit of acting virtuously.[32] In order to become kind people, we need to perform acts of kindness regularly until acting kindly becomes a habit. We can become courageous by regularly acting in the way that a courageous person would act until this develops into a habit. If this account of virtue development is right, then, we can see loyal sports fans as not only displaying but also developing the virtue of loyalty. The fans who stood by Manchester City at their lowest point not only showed their loyalty; they also further developed their habits of acting in a loyal way. By acting loyally towards their club, fans may be developing their ability to act loyally in other areas of life as well.

We might wonder, though, what is really so admirable about people who show loyalty to struggling sports teams. One reason we might question this is that it is often completely arbitrary which team people are fans of.[33] Alfred moved to Tilburg in the Netherlands for work and began to support the local team, Willem II. However, if he had moved to a different city, he would likely have started supporting an entirely different team.[34] Which team we happen to live close to is only one arbitrary factor that may determine who we support. The reason why Alfred supports Partick Thistle is that his grandmother had a friend who used to play for them, and so she said they were the team to support (despite having no interest in football herself). A child growing up in Manchester may like the color red and so decide that they like Manchester United rather than Manchester City. Given how arbitrary these choices are, why think it is virtuous for fans to show loyalty to their clubs?

One way to respond is to point out that sports fandom is not *always* arbitrary. Some fans are born into families that have supported the same team for generations. Others are born into wider communities that make it all but certain which team they will support. A Roman Catholic growing up in Glasgow, for example, is most likely to become a fan of Glasgow Celtic, if they become a fan at all. This is because Celtic are Glasgow's Catholic team, with strong historical links to the Catholic Church. The strong links to the communities these fans are part of, be it a family or a religious community, make these cases of fandom far from arbitrary.[35] However, this response only works for those whose fandom is not arbitrary.

A more general response to this worry is, again, to look at other forms of love. Many relationships that people have are the result of entirely arbitrary factors. People meet the loves of their lives because they happen to be seated together on a plane, because one delivers a pizza to the other, or because they happened to be climbing a mountain at the same time.[36]

The fact that two people met by chance does not speak against the quality of their relationship or the loyalty that they each might have for the other. As we mentioned in Chapter 1, you might fall in love with somebody for certain reasons, but you end up loving them for their particular features. In the same way, people may become fans for entirely arbitrary reasons, but that does not make the loyalty they show to their team any less admirable.[37] Luck may play a large role in making someone a fan of a team, but continuing to support the team through difficult times remains a clear demonstration of loyalty.

A different reason why we might question whether loyalty is appropriate towards sports clubs is that they are organizations rather than people. While it is clearly admirable to support people in times of need, it is far from clear why it should be admirable to provide the same kind of support to a club. People feel pain, loneliness, and abandonment – sports clubs do not. Why, then, would it be admirable to support an organization through difficult times?

One way to respond here is to say that while the club itself does not experience pain, the players, staff, and supporters do. In supporting the club, then, fans are providing support for all these people. While this response makes sense, there is something unsatisfying about it. After all, those players, staff, and especially supporters could all choose to abandon the club as well. Sacramento Kings fans and players could simply find other teams, and the staff could find other jobs. So why is it virtuous for everyone to continue supporting each other when everyone involved could simply find a different club to be involved in?

The answer relates to our argument that the whole point of fan communities is to see your team succeed. Likewise, what binds fans together with players and staff is that everyone involved in this club is engaged in a shared project of trying to make this club successful. The players are trying to win matches, the fans are trying to encourage the players, and the staff are trying to make the organization run smoothly. By continuing to support each other through difficult periods, everyone involved is showing their loyalty to each other and the shared community they have built by displaying their willingness to persist despite the setbacks.[38]

But still, we might think that there is something odd about the suffering that sports fans willingly put up with when supporting a struggling team. The pain and suffering endured by Manchester City fans when their team was relegated is not an unusual experience for partisan fans. There is a reason why long-suffering Sacramento Kings fans call their fan-website *A Royal Pain*, and it has nothing to do with the challenges faced by contemporary monarchies. In fact, the philosopher Michael Brady argues that pain and suffering are "often central to the life of the sports fan".[39] Only one team can win any given league or cup, meaning that the fans of all the other teams are likely to face disappointment. Isn't it just silly to voluntarily sign up for so much unnecessary suffering?

While it is true that sports fandom all too often leads to suffering, Brady argues that it is this same suffering that allows fans to fully appreciate sporting values and achievements.[40] For Boston Red Sox fans, the joy at winning the World Series in 2004 would have been especially intense given that they had not won it since 1918. Similarly, the joy when Manchester City won the Premier League for the first time in 2012 would have been all the more intense for those fans who witnessed the club's lowest ebb in 1998. The pain and suffering involved with sports fandom, then, are not simply unpleasant side-effects of fandom; they are a core part of what fandom is and enable fans to fully appreciate sporting success.

Moreover, Brady argues that fan suffering also serves a useful role in showing supporters who the most dedicated fans are.[41] By suffering through their team's failures and continuing to support them when times are hard, fans show each other that they possess the virtue of loyalty. Note that the point here is not only that these fans *are* loyal but that their continued fandom also *communicates* this virtue to others. This is useful as it allows fans to distinguish the genuinely committed partisan fans from the glory hunters, the fair weather fans, and the purists. The suffering that fans of losing teams undergo, then, enables fans to identify the truly committed members of the fan community. It allows the fan community to differentiate who they can trust to stick with the team from those who will leave when times are hard. Fans of the Sacramento Kings can easily identify who their loyal fans are by looking at who continues to support the team despite their long 16-year losing streak. This also benefits the individual fans, since being identified as a genuine fan will improve their social standing among other fans. They will be viewed as worthy of respect and esteem and find that other fans will be more likely to listen to their opinions and to defer to their judgment. It is through this shared suffering that fans demonstrate their loyalty to the group, and the fan community can identify the committed fans as distinct from the hangers on.

Relatedly, the suffering involved with sports fandom also seems to lead fans to develop stronger bonds of loyalty with each other. In 2014, the anthropologist Martha Newson led a survey study that investigated which group of English Premier League fans had the strongest bonds with each other.[42] The study found that fans of less successful teams expressed higher levels of loyalty towards their fellow fans, were more likely to view their identity as intertwined with that of their club, and even were more likely to express a willingness to sacrifice their own life to save the life of one of their team's fellow fans. The authors of the study suggest that the explanation for this is what they call the "shared dysphoria" pathway to fusion. Put in less fancy terms, shared suffering has been found to lead to closer social bonds between people. When people suffer together, they are more likely to feel a sense of shared identity with each other.[43] This helps to explain why fans of less successful teams may feel more closely bonded with each other. The fans that suffer together, stay together.

You might worry that we are defeating our own argument here. After all, in Chapter 3, we said that fans win when their team wins because the point of being in a fan community is to witness your team's success. If fans are closer together when they lose, doesn't that mean the whole point is not to win? Well, no. The point of being a fan is to witness your team succeed (though we can add here that success involves more than on-pitch victory; it might also involve exemplifying a certain style or showing courage against bigger teams). But much as a book group might meet in order to read a book, nobody thinks that's the only point: it's also about being part of a community and finding like-minded people you want to hang out with. Fans of losing teams can do well on this front!

Finally, the suffering endured by sports fans may also help to promote the virtue of humility. As City fan David Crook explains: "Being there when we were rubbish is not that important to our current Manchester City side but the humility we learnt when dealing with those experiences is what sets us apart from other 'big' clubs".[44] Watching your team when it is useless helps to guard against arrogance when your team becomes successful. Fans who have watched their teams when they were dreadful know that their club is not inherently better than others and that success can be fleeting. This humility may help these fans respond graciously in victory. They know what it is to suffer defeat and so can sympathize with opposing fans who are experiencing this suffering.

Being a partisan sports fan, then, can be an important means through which people develop the virtue of loyalty. Through standing by a team during difficult times, fans develop the skills to stand by other people in times of strife. Moreover, through suffering together, fans are able to truly appreciate their team's success, to communicate their virtue to others, to develop closer bonds with each other, and perhaps even to respond to their team's success with humility. Partisan fandom does not have to be adversarial and unpleasant; it can instead be a virtuous form of loyalty. Those looking for a romantic partner who will stick with them through thick and thin could do a lot worse than looking to fans of failing sports teams; just don't expect them to put you ahead of their team!

4.4 THE LIMITS OF LOYALTY

Loyalty is an admirable virtue. But this does not mean that loyalty has no limits. While it is good to be loyal to those we love, there comes a point when the right thing to do is to walk away. It is good to stick by a friend when they are going through hard times, but this does not mean that we should stand by friends who consistently take us for granted or abuse our trust. We should be loyal only to people and groups who are worthy of our loyalty.[45] In the same way, being loyal to a sports team is admirable, but this does not mean that sports fans should stick by their team no matter what. When a team betray their fans, take them for granted, or abuse their trust, walking away from the team might be the right thing for fans to do.[46]

Loyalty has other problems too. According to the philosophers Dean Cocking and Jeanette Kennett, loyalty towards friends can also be *morally dangerous*.[47] By this, they mean that being a loyal friend can make it more likely that one will act immorally. To show this, they give an example from the film *Death in Brunswick*. Carl is a chef who gets attacked by a co-worker, Mustafa. During the fight, Carl accidentally stabs Mustafa, who dies from the wound. Carl asks his friend Dave to help him get rid of Mustafa's body. Cocking and Kennett argue that Dave's friendship with Carl gives him a reason to help Carl here. In fact, they go so far as to call it a "requirement of close friendship".[48] This requirement is not a moral requirement — in fact, it violates moral requirements — but rather, a requirement that arises out of the friendship that Carl and Dave have with each other. In fact, in this case, friendship seems to require Dave to do something morally wrong or, at the very least, morally dubious. The bonds of loyalty we have with our friends can sometimes put us in difficult situations where we have good reason to act in immoral ways.

The relationship between fans and sports teams can be just as morally dangerous. For example, Matthew Hedges was a British PhD student who was arrested while conducting research in the United Arab Emirates (UAE), detained without trial, denied legal assistance, drugged, and subjected to prolonged periods of solitary confinement before being given a life sentence after being forced to sign a false confession.[49] He was subsequently released and granted clemency after an international outcry by the British government and human rights organizations. During Hedges' imprisonment, a number of sports journalists pointed out that the owner of Manchester City, Sheikh Mansour, was not only a member of the UAE royal family but also the deputy prime minister and the brother of the president. Many Manchester City fans responded by showing their support for their owner. As sportswriter Jonathan Wilson describes:

> Something extraordinary happened: significant numbers of Manchester City fans on social media came out in support of the legal system of Abu Dhabi. This is so bizarre it's worth reiterating. A proportion of supporters of a football club in the north-west of England decided to back the flawed legal apparatus of an oppressive regime 4,500 miles away against a British man who, whether he had been spying or not, had been treated appallingly for six months.[50]

While some fans were showing their support for the UAE's legal system, others sought to cast doubt upon the integrity of Tariq Panja, the journalist who uncovered the story for the *New York Times*, by claiming that the newspaper was biased against Manchester City. Other journalists who covered the story were accused by City fans on Twitter of lacking objectivity and of twisting the facts. We can see here the moral danger involved in fandom, as the love that City fans have for their club leads them to defend the legal system of a regime with an appalling human rights record and to accuse journalists of corruption and dishonesty.

So, if loyalty is generally good, but it can also lead fans to moral peril, what should we do? To return to Aristotle, virtues exist between two related vices, one involving a deficiency and one an excess. For example, courage is the virtue of staying true to a course of action in the face of danger. If we are too easily swayed by fear, then we are cowardly, which is a vice of deficiency. On the other hand, if we are too committed to a course of action, even when the dangers far outweigh the potential benefits, then we are reckless, which is a vice of excess. In the same way, loyalty is a virtue that involves sticking with one's relationships in the face of difficulty or sacrifice. If we are too quick to abandon these relationships, then we are disloyal. But if we stick with all our relationships, no matter how much damage they cause us, then we possess a vice of excess (perhaps we should call this fanatical loyalty). We should, then, develop the virtue of loyalty but not to the extent that we lose the ability to criticize our team or to see when our loyalty is unjustified.

Some fans are capable of maintaining some form of critical distance from their team. They are capable of cheering them on during a match and also criticizing the behavior of the club or their fellow fans. We call this form of fandom *critical fandom*. This critical form of fandom allows for loyalty but recognizes that there are limits to this – sometimes you need to criticize those you are loyal to, and other times you need to abandon them.

4.5 CONCLUSION

In this chapter, we have been considering a common worry raised about partisan forms of fandom. The worry is that partisan fandom is adversarial, that an inevitable part of having a strong attachment to a particular team will be a strong animosity towards those outside of one's community. While it is true that in extreme cases, partisan fandom can indeed lead to a strong "us and them" mentality, it can also lead people to help others. Moreover, it can both be a form of loyalty and a way of developing a more general virtue of loyalty. Of course, loyalty should not involve standing by one's relationships no matter what. Rather, a loyal friend is someone who is prepared to criticize their friend and eventually walk away from them if need be.

In fact, when a friendship deteriorates too much, walking away from the friendship may be the only way to stay true to the friendship as it used to be. The same is true for fans. While loyalty is a virtue here too, fans should be willing to take a critical distance from the team that they love – or in the case of purists, the sport that they love. Fans should not be fanatical devotees; they need to be critical fans who are willing to question their team. In the rest of the book, we will look more closely at what this involves. What should you do when your fellow fans, or your club, or even the sport you love does despicable things? Is it OK to keep being a fan?

Clive O'Connell was a very successful corporate lawyer. Unfortunately for him, his side – Chelsea – had just lost to Liverpool. Even more unfortunately for him, an interviewer was outside the stadium asking fans for their opinion on the game. O'Connell was not happy and said that Liverpool's fans were "scum, Scouse idiots … nasty, horrible people".[1] He promptly lost his job as a partner at a law firm.

Like many sports fans, O'Connell perhaps had those attitudes, and expressed them, *because* he had just been at a soccer game. Peer pressure is tempting. You might not ordinarily call people "scum" (or worse), but when thousands of other people – not just strangers, fellow people who love *your* team – chant it in the stadium, it becomes a lot easier to slip into that sort of behavior.

O'Connell is a vivid example of how sports fans can be led into saying stupid, nasty things. But we don't think O'Connell is exceptional. He's hardly the only person to say something ill-advised, to say something that they wouldn't ordinarily dream of saying, in the heat of the moment. And his behavior was relatively tame, given the bad things that can happen in and around sports. Sports fans are not exactly famous for being well behaved. In this chapter, we want to look at why this bad behavior matters for other, innocent fans.

DOI: 10.4324/9781003271277-6

There are two major concerns. The first one is that fans can be led morally astray by their fandom. We don't have any special insight into what Clive O'Connell is like as a person – but plenty of us know people who are lovely, restrained, and respectful but who become horrible, angry, and aggressive when their team loses. The first concern is that fan cultures can make people think, say, or do nasty things.

The second concern is that even if you can resist being turned to the moral dark side by your fellow fans, if other fans are behaving terribly, that reflects badly on you. Even if you resist sliding down the slippery slope into the moral mire, the stench carries.

Our argument in the first part of this book was that there are many upsides to fandom, even if there are downsides. All things considered, fandom can often be worthwhile. This chapter and the next grant that it's OK to be a fan. In fact, it's often very good. But sometimes, it isn't OK. You could say that the rest of the book is concerned with another question: *when* is it OK to be a sports fan? To put it more concretely, we'll be looking at questions such as these. Why does it matter when fellow fans are violent? How should fans react when their star player is accused of assault? What are the moral risks of fandom that fans need to be aware of?

And we'll look at a follow-up question, too: *what should you do* when it isn't OK to be a sports fan … but you are a fan? So in the rest of this book, we aren't just concerned with sketching the moral issues; we want to look at how they affect fans and what fans should do.

In the first part of this chapter, we'll explore the moral risks associated with the misdeeds of fellow fans. In response, we'll develop further the idea of *critical fandom* that we're going to be building upon for the rest of this book. We'll suggest two sorts of response critical fans might adopt: sometimes we should abandon our fandom, and at other times we should change how we engage with our team. In the next chapter, we'll talk about the moral risks that owners, players, and sports introduce, and we'll think about how the critical fan should respond there.

5.1 FANS, CRIMES, AND MISBEHAVIOR

So, what sort of moral failures by fellow fans do we have in mind? Although there are other issues that might arise (such as when fans use homophobic slurs or the classism inherent in Clive O'Connell's rant[2]), we want to focus on three: violence, racism, and sexism.

5.1.1 Violence

Unfortunately, there's no place better to start than with the British soccer hooligans or the Italian ultras, both of which are organized groups of fans that have a reputation for violence and for clashing with fan groups from rival teams.[3] These fans have reputations for indulging in horrendous behavior – a bit like the *barras bravas* from Chapter 4 who erupted in the Liga MX game in March, 2022. We will focus on that bad behavior, but first, it is worth pointing out that sometimes ultras and hooligans are caricatured or turned into some sort of moral panic. After all, we want to focus on a real issue, not an unfair stereotype.

The sociologist Gary Armstrong spent some time in the 1990s immersed in a group of football hooligans and wrote a vivid depiction of these "Blades" hooligans – hooligan fans of Sheffield United FC. Armstrong gives an in-depth documentation of the activities of the Blades over several years.[4] It's clear from his work that hooligans are not just random groups of lads engaging in mindless violence. Hooligans form societies within the broader society of fans, and they follow rules which make it clear that they should only be violent to *other* hooligan groups, rather than to ordinary fans.[5] Armstrong also makes a strong case that much of their behavior has been misrepresented and sensationalized by the press, politicians, and academics.

Ultras are also far more complex than the violent bullies they are often portrayed as. The journalist and author Tobias Jones, who has written a book on ultras,[6] notes that Cosenza's ultras have opened food banks, created play-parks for disabled kids, and are deeply anti-fascist (as opposed to many other ultra groups).[7] And in Belarus, several different groups of ultras have banded together to fight against the autocratic Lukashenko regime – at great personal risk. Some, forced to flee the country, have sought refuge with ultra groups in neighboring countries, showing how there can be a solidarity between fans that crosses club allegiances.[8]

Yet, the caricatures have some grounding, and ultras and hooligans are deeply associated with violence. For instance, hooligans might throw things at each other, hit each other with pool cues, or indulge in city-wide fights where they chase each other through the streets before or after the game.[9] Ultras are also renowned for their violence. Take the following, from Jones:

> As the ultras grew in influence, the number of people injured inside and outside football stadiums increased from 400 in the 1995–96 season to 1,200 in 1999–2000. The names of "martyrs" of ultra-related violence could often be seen spray-painted on the walls of cities across Italy. There were tributes to both ultra members

Why It's OK to Be a Sports Fan

and regular fans: Claudio Spagnolo (knifed on his way to a match); Vincenzo Paparelli (who died when a nautical rocket fired by an ultra flew the length of the pitch and hit him in the head); Antonio De Falchi (a Roma fan murdered outside the stadium); Antonio Currò (killed when a Catania fan threw a homemade bomb into a group of Messina fans); Sergio Ercolano (who fell to his death in 2003).[10]

What unites both hooligans and ultras is that these are organized subsections of deeply committed fans. And some groups of these fans regularly engage in sickening violence.

But violence is not just limited to organized bands in soccer. Fans in all sorts of sports can indulge in various forms of violence, and often spontaneously: from charging the field and injuring players and fans, to fighting each other, or just wantonly throwing objects – which might be aimed at disrupting the game but can always hit an innocent bystander. Much of this seems to just erupt: it isn't one group of hooligans searching the streets for another or meeting at a certain place for a fight; it's that something happens in the game or the stands, and then the violence kicks off. Basketball games have descended into violence among the players, with fans quickly joining in.[11] Baseball fans are not above throwing objects onto the field.[12] Low-level soccer games can descend into fans throwing seats at each other.[13] Football fans fight, leading police to attempt to defuse the problem with pepper balls.[14] Even *cricket* can be afflicted by fan violence. In 2001, hundreds of fans charged onto the pitch as England played Pakistan, and a steward suffered broken ribs.[15] These are just some examples: you can find many more on a long Wikipedia list dedicated to violence among spectators.[16] And that list only goes back to 1879; it doesn't include the long history of sporting violence. The Nika riots in 532 AD were partly sparked by the planned execution of some fans who themselves had rioted during a chariot race and – in doing so – murdered people.[17] You don't have to pay attention to sporting fandom for long to get more than your fill of blood.

What problem does this violence raise for those non-violent fans who just want to enjoy the game, and how should they respond to this? As we suggested earlier, there are two main concerns: one is that the upstanding fans will gradually slip into bad behavior, and the other is that, even if they avoid this, it reflects badly on them. Innocent fans might *become* violent, and fellow fans being violent should bring *shame* on even the non-violent fans. We'll come back to these concerns shortly, but first, we need to deal with two other blights: racism and sexism.

5.1.2 Racism

Fans of the NFL's Kansas City Chiefs and the MLB's Atlanta Braves (more on those names in the next chapter) – as well as several other teams – have a celebration where they move their arms up and down (perhaps holding a foam tomahawk), pretending to be a Native American. The problem with "the tomahawk chop" is obvious: these fans are reducing Native Americans – who have been treated abysmally by other Americans for centuries – to ridiculous, violent *caricatures*. This is deeply demeaning.

We aren't exactly offering a new, insightful criticism here: this practice has been criticized for at least 30 years.[18] And if you aren't familiar with this practice, it isn't like the racist chants you might get in a soccer game, which are – typically – from a small section of supporters. Rather, most of the stadium will join in. The racist mockery is widespread, it pervades the stands.

What about those racist soccer chants we just mentioned? You can barely go two weeks without a story breaking about racism from fans in a top-flight soccer league. Fans of the Italian soccer team Lazio – especially their ultras – are renowned for their antisemitism directed at their rivals, Roma (who historically have a relatively large portion of Jewish fans); in the late 1990s, Lazio fans held up a banner directed to Roma fans that read "Auschwitz Is Your Country; the Ovens Are Your Homes".[19] Fans of rival teams of Tottenham Hotspur (another club with a Jewish fanbase) sometimes hiss, imitating the sound of the gas chambers used in the Holocaust.[20] There are too many incidents to list of fans making monkey noises or throwing bananas at Black players. This, again, isn't just confined to soccer, with, for instance, Black NBA players being abused by Utah Jazz fans.[21]

5.1.3 Sexism

Sexism exists among sports fans, too. This is not a surprise, with sports having historically been an important focus of masculinity.[22] The philosopher Erin Tarver has argued that men want to keep women out of sports because if men are using sports fandom as a way of bonding with other men and expressing their masculinity, the "effectiveness of this form of sports participation as a homosocial institution is … in question when women enter it".[23] So, men test women, quizzing them to make sure they know specific facts about sports, or they assume that women are sporting idiots.

Tarver quotes the tale of the sports broadcaster ESPN's anchor Linda Cohn, who joked that the Red Sox beat the Yankees by a touchdown. Cohn *obviously* knows that these are baseball teams and a touchdown is from American Football. She's an anchor on a sports network! But several men contacted the station to say that she clearly didn't know sports.[24] This experience fits a more general pattern among women sports fans. In a study of female soccer and rugby fans in England conducted by the sociologist Stacey Pope, many reported feeling the need to prove that they were authentic fans.[25] At the same time, many of these fans were clear that they were not interested in more stereotypically female activities, such as watching soap operas. In Pope's view, the desire to show that they were not interested in these more traditionally female activities was motivated by a desire to show that they were genuine sports fans. This is a response to "the existing stereotypes or assumptions of women as inferior or inauthentic sports fans".[26]

Tarver gets it spot on when she says that the practices of demanding that women prove their authenticity as sports fans "convey a clear message to women fans: you don't belong here".[27] Even if sports are an important way for men to bond, it should be clear that the value of sports fandom is there for everybody.

Unfortunately, being labeled as inauthentic and being excluded in these ways is far from the only form of sexism that women face in fan environments. In a survey of English women soccer fans conducted in 2021, 20% of women fans attending men's matches reported that they had experienced unwanted physical attention. Only 37% of the women who took the survey said that they hadn't witnessed any sexist behavior from other fans.[28] To give a couple of examples of just how bad things can be, here are two cases sent in by listeners to the *Guardian Football Weekly* in an episode focused on misogyny in football.

We warn readers here that these cases are unpleasant reports of sexual assault and sexual harassment, so feel free to skip to the next section, "The responsibilities of fans", if you would prefer not to read these.

Worst thing that ever happened was when I was standing on the Kop. I must have been about 17 or 18 at the time. We were always packed in tight with everyone else so you got used to being up close with other people who were mainly men. I was wearing a red waterproof jacket and when I went to put my hand in my pocket, the man just behind and to the side of me had put his penis in there. His mates found my reaction to accidentally touching it hysterically funny but I don't think I ever wore that jacket again. At the time it was just seen as something unpleasant that happened so nobody suggested reporting it. I don't think I could have done anything anyway as I was in the middle of the Kop and wouldn't have found him again to point out the culprit. It was very much a masculine environment at the time.

Before the pandemic, my sister and I used to go to about five home games a season. In general, our experience was positive apart from not being able to see much when everyone was standing. However, on one occasion a few years ago when we were in our early twenties but looked younger, we went to a Boxing Day derby game against West Ham. After the game, we decided to walk some of the way back but in some unfortunate timing ended up heading straight into the opposition fans leaving the stadium. We kept our heads down and started to quietly make our way home but were horrified to hear a chant taken up that was clearly meant at the two of us alone, "These two take it up the arse". It rippled and repeated several times across the fans and several laughed. Clearly they had no idea or didn't care how aggressive and intimidating they seemed. As two young brown women in a sea of hundreds of opposition fans, we did what many women would have done and stayed silent and tried to hurry home. However, part of me still regrets not saying anything and standing up for my sister.[29]

These are awful examples of how sexism pervades sports. From jibes and jokes, to an inability to believe that women can be experts in sport, to physical assault, sexism is a blight among sports fans. Though this is not the place for an in-depth analysis of this sexism, it should be clear that many men make sports fandom an unwelcoming arena for women (and in the next chapter, we will see how they perpetuate the sexism present in the *sports themselves*, too).

5.2 THE RESPONSIBILITIES OF FANS

These are just some examples of the bad behavior fans can engage in. Our aim here is to give you a few examples; we expect (alas) that most of you will have many more, from the sports you love or the teams you support. Not all sports will be the same, not all fan groups will behave so badly, but the risk of violence, racism, and sexism is endemic to virtually all sports. And in some sports, or for some groups of fans, this bad behavior is almost inescapable: you can't go to a Kansas City Chiefs game without tens of thousands of people around you taking part in some humiliating racist cosplay.

Of course, it is wrong to take part in this behavior. But what about fans who *don't* engage in violence and racism – how should they respond to it? And why do they even need to respond to it in the first place?

One potential response from fans is that these violent fans (or these racists, or sexists) is that they aren't *real* fans. This is just violence, and it has nothing to do with sport. Several of the violent incidents we discussed in the previous chapter were one-offs caused by various socio-political elements combined to create an explosive environment. Perhaps it is easy enough to say that these sorts of events have nothing much to do with *sports fandom*; it is just that a bunch of people, already tense, were in the same area, and if sports hadn't set things off, something else would have. But it is not so easy to offer this response when sports are clearly central to the violence: when it is *fans* who are violent solely *because they are fans* – motivated by love of their team and hatred of the other – not because, say, they are patriots defending their national honor. Those are the cases we were looking at in this chapter.

Still, there is *something* to be said for the argument that *some* of these people aren't really sports fans. For instance, Gary Armstrong's account of the Blades looks at how they would travel to the city where United were playing and meet up with rival hooligans before fighting with these total strangers.[30] They would also meet fans of United's major rivals – Sheffield Wednesday – on Friday and Saturday evenings to fight. You might think that in these cases, fighting is what matters. If football is merely a convenient way to schedule gang fights, are these hooligans really sports fans, or do they just piggyback on the club's calendar? So, too, with ultras. Tobias Jones thinks that for many ultras, football doesn't really matter: "Being an ultra isn't about watching the football, but watching each other: admiring the carnival on the curva [in the stands], not the game on the grass".[31]

This riposte might work against *some* badly behaved "fans". Yet, it only goes so far. Even if *some* hooligans and ultras are just in it for violence or (more innocently) some sort of boys' club, it is abundantly clear from both Armstrong's and Jones's work that many others *are* deeply committed fans: it really matters to them that their team wins, and they want to be there to see it.

To try to claim that these fans are not real fans reeks of the *no true Scotsman* fallacy. This fallacy involves claiming that no *real* Scotsman would do such a thing (for instance, cheer on England) – even if a Scotsman is doing such a thing. The Scotsman who cheers on England is indeed a Scotsman; he's just doing something that some other Scots really don't like. Likewise, to claim that these hooligans and ultras aren't real fans doesn't seem to be true: they are fans, they're just doing something other fans are repelled by. They're nasty fans (often), but they're still fans. So, even if we might be able to claim that some who claim to be fans aren't really fans – they're just there for violence, not for sports – the argument doesn't hold good for, say, the cricket fans who rushed the pitch, the basketball fans spewing hate, or the soccer fans hissing at historically Jewish opponents.

Given the limits of that argument, here is a second response that innocent fans might offer when faced by a section of disreputable fans. They might grant that even if these fans are part of the same community, that shouldn't matter: so long as I do not misbehave, why does it matter that these other fans are misbehaving?

Well, we've given the spoilers to this question at the start of the chapter. (Philosophy makes for a bad murder mystery – it's all about the journey.) There are two big problems with this response. Here's the first one: who you associate with affects how you see the world. We saw in Chapter 1 that when you are in love with someone (or something, like a sports club), that affects how you see the world; it's also true that who you associate with affects how you see the world. Take the example we started this chapter with, Clive O'Connell. It wouldn't surprise us if the respectable lawyer O'Connell had been desensitized to the wrongness of calling people "scum" just by being at the game. O'Connell didn't spew racism, but he was bigoted in some other way – and we can easily see how the same sort of slippage could occur that allows a fan to slip into racism or violence, even if they would do no such thing if it were not for the hundreds of other fans doing the same.

The fact that this can happen should not surprise anybody. As we pointed out in Chapter 2, sports fandom offers a wonderful outlet for our emotions – emotions that often need to be stifled in everyday life. The worry is that as we loosen our inhibitions, we may be losing the part of our psychology that helps us to act in a morally acceptable way. This might also lead us to miss morally important facts: some fans might not recognize that doing the tomahawk chop is racist. Whereas outside the stadium they might recognize that pretending to be Native Americans is problematic (alas, some might not see this), when thousands of other fans are doing something wrong, it might seem more acceptable, harder to resist. After all, it's easier to do something bad – or to think it isn't bad – if those around you are also behaving badly. So, that's one reason why it matters that there are bad apples: they can turn others bad, too. They spoil the barrel. Good fans can't just ignore the bad fans, because the bad fans put them in moral peril – the bad fans might make the good fans bad.

The second problem is that awful fans *reflect* the whole community – including innocent fans. Guilt is based on *what we ourselves do*, so it doesn't make sense to feel guilty about what these other fans have done. But guilt does not exhaust the moral reactions we might have to bad behavior: there is also *shame*. During Euro 2020, some England fans behaved appallingly. Ahead of the final, thousands stormed Wembley Stadium, security staff were assaulted, and a young woman was pushed to the ground and trampled.[32] One fan, who also got into Wembley without a ticket, shoved a lit flare up his arse.[33] Even if this isn't exactly violent, it's probably not the sort of family-friendly behavior we want to encourage at major sporting events. (It might set something off.) The Wembley incident was horrendous, but this was no one-off. These fans travel to away games, sing sectarian chants, and get arrested for violence in the cities they stay in. As an England fan, Jake is ashamed of this behavior. This is a form of *collective shame*, in which fans identify with a collective, in this case the England fans, which they view to be shameful.[34]

Let's explore this shame in a little more depth. We argued in Chapters 2 and 3 that being a partisan fan is often worthwhile *because* you are part of a community – a community that gives meaning to your life and shapes your identity. Sure, some fans may be able to reap these benefits through solitary engagement with their team, but many partisans have such a deep engagement with their teams precisely because they are part of such communities. That serves as a great defense against the claim that partisan fandom is meaningless or stupid. But it is a double-edged sword: the community can be a source of meaning, and it can also be a source of great moral risk. It means that when groups of fans misbehave, *your community* might be misbehaving, and that reflects on you.

While guilt attaches to our actions, pride and shame can be responses to what we *identify with*. We can feel proud or ashamed of ourselves, members of our family, our friends, or our cities or nations (or of course, the teams we love).

Imagine two people. Ross isn't particularly interested in what his country does; Steve takes great pride in all of his country's achievements. Ross is perfectly consistent if he also doesn't feel any great shame over his nation's misdeeds. He doesn't identify with his country, so he doesn't feel any pride or shame. But if Steve, who is proud when his country excels, doesn't feel pangs of shame when his country does something awful, it seems that he is being inconsistent. He wants to identify with his country, but only in a disingenuous and half-hearted way: only insofar as it benefits him. Yet even if he doesn't feel shame, if he identifies with his country and takes pride in its actions, then those misdeeds do in fact reflect on him – he should feel shame, and others (a bit more attuned to moral reality, a bit less egotistical) will think less of him both for what his country does and for his failure to feel appropriately ashamed.

The same is true with sports fans. We are interested here in the moral issues of fandom, but there is also a parallel here with what some have called BIRGing: Basking In Reflected Glory.[35] This is when a fan glories in the fact their team has won. We think we have made a pretty convincing case for why, actually, the fan succeeds when the team succeeds, in Chapter 3. But even though we think many fans rightly glory in victory, some fans do BIRG: they might not identify with the team enough and only care about the team when they are winning (they're "fair weather fans").[36] What might trouble us about such fans is that they identify with the team only selectively: they aren't there for the bad times, the relegations, the winless seasons; they are there only for the wins. They have no loyalty.

As well as BIRGing, these fans might CORF: they might Cut Off Reflected Failure.[37] Fair weather fans seem to naturally CORF: they are there only for the glory, not the failures. Our concern is with the fans who are genuinely committed to the team, who glory in victory and are upset by defeat. The concern here isn't the usual one, that they CORF when it comes to *sporting* failures. The fans we are worried about CORF when it comes to *moral* failures: they accept that they are part of a sporting community that lends meaning to their lives, but they cut off the elements that are morally troubling. It's like being a committed American patriot who thinks the way that the American political system has victimized Black Americans isn't your problem; it's like being a dedicated, flag-waving Brit who ignores the stain of colonialism. If you want to say your community succeeds, you better be willing to say your community can fail.

What should be clear is that there are two sides to the coin here. For one, bad fans are still *fans*. So good fans can't just cut off the bad guys by saying that they are not really fans. On the other side, good fans can't cut themselves off from the group by saying that these moral failings aren't their problem. There are two reasons why they can't simply say these bad fans aren't their problem. The first is that the bad fans provide the good fans with a moral risk: the good fans might be influenced to do bad. The second is that to dissociate is a moral form of CORFing, and if fans want to be able to succeed when their team and its community succeed, they have to take the rough with the smooth.

Our point is not that fans have no way of *pushing away* these disreputable fans. It is to underline why this must be done in the right way. These violent or racist fans *are part of the same community*. But fans are not inert; they are not forced to simply accept or ignore this bad behavior. They can avoid the moral taint of abysmal fans *and* resist the slide into immoral behavior themselves. But how?

5.3 CRITICAL FANDOM

5.3.1 The idea of a critical fan

Our suggestion is that fans should engage in *critical fandom*, which we briefly mentioned in the last chapter. To be a critical fan requires some nuance – but it is the sort of nuance we think is within reach of any ordinary fan. We saw in Chapter 3 that partisan fans are able to appreciate the great moments of skill and excitement that the opposition team might produce. Fans also boo their own side sometimes, recognizing that even though it is *their* team, the team they support, they are doing badly. It's this sort of nuance that critical fandom requires: if you can admit the other side might be good, if you can admit your side can be bad, you should also be able to admit that your own fellow fans can sometimes be *morally* bad. And this recognition is followed by another: that you can do something about this, either by changing your behavior or by changing *how* you are a fan. And at the limits, this can include abandoning your fandom, ceasing to be a fan.

Being a critical fan is a bit like being a critical friend or family member. Good family members don't let their family members get away with *terrible* behavior. Good friends care about each other, and this includes caring that their friends are not becoming awful people. Good friends will criticize their friends – sometimes gently, sometimes not so gently – for their racist tirades or other bad behavior. They'll try to set a good example to their friends and encourage them to be better people.[38] If none of this works, then eventually a good friend may have to withdraw from the friendship altogether. If, for example, your friend group become scheming murderers, then it is probably a good idea to try to find new friends.

The idea of a critical fan, like being a good critical friend or family member, is *an ideal* – we certainly aren't saying that this is how all friends or family members *are*; we are saying it is how they *should be*. In Donna Tartt's novel *The Secret History*, the protagonist Richard takes an alternative approach to friendship: he finds out that his friends have killed somebody and then joins in as they plot to kill somebody else. Richard is friends with these other people, even if the friendship has some weird power imbalances; but he is not a critical friend – he is a snob and a try-hard, who wants to be accepted by this elite group, so he accepts their behavior and goes along with it. Were he a critical friend, he might have tried to prevent their second heinous act, or he might have turned them in to the authorities and abandoned them.

The notion of a critical friend goes alongside the recognition that friendship is very important, and it should not be easily disposed of.[39] But critical friends notice that if something is important it should be valued *appropriately*, and if it starts to tarnish, those tarnishes need to be addressed; and if it is too flawed, it might no longer be valuable at all. Richard's case in *The Secret History* is clear cut: it becomes obvious that the friendships he has are deeply toxic and bad for him and those around him.

But it isn't always clear what the critical friend needs to do. Dave, Carl's friend in *Death in Brunswick*, seems to have two choices. He can either help Carl dispose of the body, or he can tell Carl that he has gone too far. It may not always be clear what the right approach is: *sometimes*, being a good friend might be more important than being a morally upstanding person. If Carl was unfortunate and didn't mean to kill Mustafa, it might be worth standing up for him and helping him, rather than turning him over to the machinations of an uncaring and unloving legal system – even if this is illegal or perhaps even immoral.

Though we don't pretend there are always clear rules that say what a critical friend should do, we can see some general principles. Critical friends will criticize wrongdoing; they will try to prevent it. If their friend starts planning a murder, they will talk them out of it. If their friend is an unrepentant racist, they will try to show them what is wrong with this. Sometimes, though, they may have to disassociate themselves from their friends altogether. The position we are committed to here is a broad one: that critical friends must sometimes abandon their friends if they become terrible people. This leaves a lot of room to still be friends with bad people, to try to improve them, or perhaps just to tolerate their awful traits due to the strong and loving connection you have. The same is true when it comes to critical fandom.

This critical fandom requires us to be critical both of fellow fans and – as we'll move on to in the next chapter – of the sports and clubs we love. Like with critical friendship, what exactly critical fandom requires of us will depend on the case: it will depend on the nature of an individual's fandom, it will depend on the way that the bad behavior relates to the club, the sport, or the fan community, and it will depend on what exactly that bad behavior was. A relatively uncommitted or fledgling fan might, in the face of awful behavior by other fans, need to give up their fandom – whereas we cannot expect that from a lifelong fan. After all, the lifelong fan's fandom is more valuable than the fledgling's, so it's more of a cost for her to give up her fandom. Abandonment might sometimes be on the table even for some lifelong fans, but we also can't expect fans to abandon their clubs over every minor moral wrongdoing.

Critical fandom tells you to treat your fandom with a critical eye. It requires that even though you are loyal, you are willing to take a basic critical stance where you will criticize your team or your fellow fans for wrongdoing. But it doesn't prescribe specific actions that apply in every case, because there are so many forms of fandom and so many forms of bad behavior.[40] Sometimes, it is clear what a critical friend should do (like in Richard's case, where it is clear he should take action; it's just that he fails to be critical and do the right thing). We aren't saying that being a critical fan is easy!

With that in mind, what can we say about the violence, sexism, and racism we have discussed in this chapter? Here are two broad things critical fans can do: they can withdraw their fandom, and they can transform the way that they are fans.[41]

5.3.2 Withdrawal

Withdrawing fandom, abandoning your team, is clearly an extreme move. The argument of this book is that being a sports fan is not just OK; rather, it's often very valuable for people. So, to withdraw this comes at some great costs: you abandon that very valuable fandom. Likewise, although friendship is valuable, sometimes things are so bad that you must abandon your friend.

Yet sometimes, abandonment can solve the root problem. In 2021, Raith Rovers Football (soccer) Club in Scotland announced the signing of David Goodwillie – who had previously been found (by a civil court) to have raped a woman.[42] Rovers' main sponsor, lifelong fan Val McDermid, said she would be withdrawing her support; several members of the women's team, including the captain, resigned; workers at the club – from directors to stadium announcers – criticized the club, and swathes of fans said they would no longer support the club. The mass abandonment by fans, players, and directors of Raith Rovers after they signed Goodwillie solved the problem they were protesting: they objected to the club signing Goodwillie, and the club then went back on their decision.[43]

Even if fans are not willing to abandon their own fandom, they may engage in a form of intergenerational withdrawal when they decide that, say, they are not willing to take their children to their team's matches. In Glasgow, the fierce rivalry between Rangers and Celtic and the associated bigotry and violence have led some fans to decide to take their fans to see other teams instead, such as Partick Thistle. These children then develop an attachment to the club they are watching and become Partick Thistle fans, even if their parents remain fans of Rangers or Celtic. This is a form of withdrawal even though it does not involve anyone giving up their own fandom: the parents can still be fans of their club while recognizing the moral problems with such fandom and keeping their children away from it.

But withdrawing fandom is less likely to have a practical impact when the problem comes from *fellow fans* – which is what we have been discussing in this chapter. Sure, fans could put pressure on the club to try to stamp out some of these issues (like racist fan chanting), but good fans withdrawing their fandom doesn't seem to be an effective way of making bad fans behave appropriately. That is because these bad fans will often be less reliant on other fans remaining fans – whereas sports teams, especially smaller ones, might feel more of an impact if fans withdraw.

Yet even if the practical effect is limited, it might still be an important move, grounded in a fan's own self-respect and principles, to withdraw their fandom and thus their association with racists, bigots, and hooligans. When it comes to abandoning fandom due to the bad behavior of fellow fans, the driving force seems to be that it's *too much for you* to keep being associated with these people, even if abandoning your fandom comes at great personal cost. Someone who once felt pride in being American might think that systemic racism brings too much shame and he'd rather no longer take pride in America because he cannot support what it does; Dave might think he could forgive Carl for many things, but not for murder; and a Lazio fan might, after hearing vile antisemitic chants from fellow supporters for years, not be able to stomach it any more once he sees the disgraceful antisemitic banner we mentioned earlier.

5.3.3 Transformation

Yet there is a less extreme response to fellow bad fans than abandonment, and it is often a step that we think should be tried first. Rather than abandoning your fandom, you might want to try to change the bad behavior – or, if you can't do that, at least change how you engage in your fandom so that you can *appropriately* insulate yourself from that behavior.

This is when fans *transform* their fandom. There are many ways that fans might do this, but here is one possibility. Turkish soccer club Beşiktaş's "Çarşı" ultras are left-wing and anti-racist. When Samuel Eto'o suffered racist abuse (in a game in Spain, not involving Beşiktaş), they raised a banner saying "We are all Samuel Eto'o".[44] This is just one small gesture against the weight of racism in European soccer, but we can see how this can be an effort to persuade other fans to behave properly, and if that fails, it is a step to appropriately disassociating from *bad fans*. If a sport or a club is afflicted with a virulent and vocal group of racist fans, what is to stop another group of fans distancing themselves from them *by setting up their own group*, a group that opposes racism and hatred?

By setting up a group that explicitly opposes such behavior, they try to show that there is another, better, way of being a fan, and they dissociate from the racist (or violent) fans in a *principled* way. They aren't just saying "Those fans aren't like us" by waving their hands in a vague, unsubstantiated manner. Instead, they are setting up their own ethical principles and saying "This is what our fans *should be like*, join us, not them!"

Further, these fans help to inoculate themselves against losing their own moral values: by associating with fellow anti-racist fans who affirm that good behavior, fans protect themselves from moral slippage. The fans who associate with others who firmly oppose racism should be much less likely to slip into the trap like the one that caught Clive O'Connell because they aren't surrounded by the temptation of bad behavior. And by doing this, fans would also be explicitly condemning the bad behavior in a public way. This would reduce another lurking worry about associating with other fans who misbehave: you might be seen to condone their behavior.[45] We haven't addressed this issue yet, as we'll talk about related issues in the next chapter.

This is just one way that fans can transform the way that they are fans. There are other transformational steps that a fan might take in the face of other fans being racist or violent, and the transformation here might be relatively low-key, like changing where you sit and how you engage with others. Despite our reservations about fans using the simplistic "Well, why should what they do reflect on *me*?" excuse, there clearly are subgroups of fans, and fans can take powerful steps here. If it turns out that the fans who engage in racist chanting sit in a certain area, and it's the area that you sit in, you should move away from them – get your seats elsewhere next time. Or take a stand and *literally* turn your back on them!

Fans can also take other personal, individual steps to move away – both physically and in terms of signaling disapproval – from bad fans. If you're tailgating before the game, and someone you're sharing a few beers with makes an off-color or racially loaded comment, you might want to tell them that such behavior isn't appropriate. Sometimes, this can be effective, especially if they are your friend and you are a critical friend as well as a critical fan. But even if this fails, making it clear to fellow fans what sort of standards of behavior are appropriate can be a straightforward first step in taking action. It won't stop the racist chanting, it won't stop the violence, but it might thin out the ranks of people – perhaps like Clive O'Connell – whose fandom leads them to allow their standards to slip.

Fans can also look at other, broader modes of transformation that are targeted at revolutionizing the entire way they engage in fandom, rather than seeking to just respond to a particular problem. Fans of Beşiktaş again provide us with another model of transformation. The Ladies of Beşiktaş were formed in 2006.[46] Passionate football fans, they

> reject the dominant culture of football fandom, and are unwilling to repress their femininity. They are open about being wives/girlfriends and mothers. They attend games dressed in identical black and white scarves and jackets. Initially, they sat together at games, but no longer make a point of doing so. They blow whistles when fans are heard using insulting language; this, naturally, includes (but is not confined to) sexist, racist and homophobic language. They propose a different fan culture.[47]

These fans have had an impact on the broader fan culture, moderating the bad behavior of unruly male fans. Turkey has seen other transformative fan reactions. After a stadium ban for a pitch invasion, Fenerbahçe were allowed to play in front of women and children. The other team was greeted not with a cauldron of animosity, but with *flowers*.[48] Fans of rival clubs were invited to watch, too – something that would be unimaginable had the stadium been filled with traditional, male-dominated fan groups. We aren't saying that these changes bring us towards a perfect, blemish-free fandom, but these changes show that we can move towards a transformed model of fandom founded on *support*, not on animosity or hatred.

Whatever way that critical fans decide to respond – whether to instances of bad behavior or in a more wholesale way – we hope that it is clear that fans sometimes face a moral imperative to change how they engage when fellow fans are awful. And we also hope that the examples of transformation we have sketched seem *possible*: they are the sort of steps we can realistically see fans taking. Critical fans do not need to be resigned to fighting a losing battle, always accepting the bad behavior of others. They might not be able to stop the bad behavior, but perhaps sometimes they can. And if they cannot stop it, they can engage in other modes of fandom that insulate them from these bad fans.

5.4 CONCLUSION

There will be limits to how critical any fan should be. We are suggesting that fans should be moderately critical, not that they should turn into moralistic scolds. Nobody is perfect, no fan group will be perfect, and attempting to blot out every little speck of imperfection will be immensely annoying. If, in the pursuit of moral purity, you are too much of a zealot, you risk doing harm by trying to stop people from enjoying something meaningful, one which is mostly harmless from a moral perspective. In the same way, a good friend or a family member wouldn't point our every little flaw in your behavior.

Here is what we mean. Fans of the Buffalo Bills call themselves the Bills Mafia (and the players and club use this term for their fans, too). Jake doesn't like that. He thinks it probably glorifies organized crime and is at best a bit tacky. Jake will, sometimes, complain about this to friends, and he won't use the term or buy "Bills Mafia" merchandise. But, really, who cares? It's not racist (even if one *might* argue that it uses damaging Italian-American stereotypes).[49] His inclination is that this isn't enough of a moral issue to do anything much about. And he has good reason to think he's not just being a coward who is avoiding a righteous moral fight: there is little criticism of this name in the public media (whereas the chop is rightly criticized often enough), and he hopes that this is because it genuinely is much less of an issue. Were he to point out how awful the name was every time he saw it used on Twitter or when watching a game, it would simply be annoying – and be annoying not in the service of a righteous moral fight but over a relatively minor thing.

We need to pick our battles, and sometimes we need to just put up with some minor bad fan behavior. This will be a judgment we have to make, and sometimes we might get it wrong by overreacting to minor imperfections or shying away from genuine issues that need to be confronted. But the general point here is that not every minor imperfection requires a big response.

On the other hand, it's worth emphasizing that our argument is not that being a critical fan is *easy*.[50] It is tempting to overlook the flaws of our fellow fans, much as it is tempting to overlook the flaws of those we love. As the philosopher Francisco Javier López Frías points out, some theories hold that fans are "so emotionally bounded to those who belong to their group" that they can't behave appropriately – but he rightly argues that this goes too far.[51] Even when we are partial towards those on our side, we still can be expected to behave appropriately to other people, even those on the other side.

When we recognize these flaws, we must not simply ignore them or dissociate ourselves from them. If being part of a fan community is important to you, you can't simply decide to reap the benefits and ignore the fact that how others behave reflects on you and can tempt you into bad behavior. Sometimes, you have to do something about it. And if you fail to do that, you risk being tarnished by the behavior of these racist fellow fans – or even *becoming* one of the racists, slipping down the moral slide in spite of yourself.

Ben Roethlisberger played for the Pittsburgh Steelers for nearly 20 years. He has been accused of sexual assault, though he has never been charged in court. Recently, the Cleveland Browns signed Deshaun Watson on a blockbuster deal despite being aware of allegations from over 20 women that he had sexually harassed or assaulted them while they were giving him professional massages. He has been banned for 11 games but still has a contract worth hundreds of millions of dollars. Within the last year, several English Premier League soccer players have been accused of or charged with rape or assault.

Of course, not all of these cases end up leading to criminal conviction. Yet even when there is no conviction, fans may still have difficult choices to make. After all, we make moral judgments all the time that would not necessarily meet legal standards for criminal conviction. You might not hang out with someone who was credibly accused of doing something awful if he escaped punishment on a technicality or through good lawyering. Nor do we need to bicker about individual cases. What matters is that *sometimes*, a sportsperson will have done something very bad – and we'll be able to make that judgment with a reasonable degree of certainty, even if a legal case wouldn't stick. Other times, a player will be found by a court to have done something awful yet will return to the sport. Our question in this chapter is how fans should

DOI: 10.4324/9781003271277-7

respond when a player, their club, or even their entire sport is engaged in wrongdoing.

Just as when fellow fans behave badly, bad behavior from players can tempt the good fans to do bad – we, rightly or wrongly, look up to players as role models – and bad behavior from players associated with a team should arouse shame in that team's fans.[1] But there are distinct moral concerns for fans when the object of their fandom – the player, the club, the sport that they love – is morally awful. To start, we are going to look at cases where fans actively *support* this wrongdoing. Then, we are going to move on to cases where fans don't necessarily support something wrong; rather, they are, perhaps through no fault of their own, *complicit* in it.

6.1 SUPPORT

6.1.1 The problem of support

In early 2022, Manchester United's Mason Greenwood was accused by a former girlfriend of sexual assault and making death threats.[2] There was video evidence, along with audio clips of Greenwood, suggesting that he had done and said some disgusting, violent things. Yet, plenty of fans rallied to his support. Twitter was awash with this. To take just one example, one fan posted:

> If Mason Greenwood has million fans, then I'm one of them. If Mason Greenwood has 5 fans I'm one of them. If Mason Greenwood has one fan, then I'm THAT ONE. If Mason Greenwood has no fans, that means I'm dead. If the world is againt Mason Greenwood than im against the world.[3]

This is Twitter, so it's possible that this is just some troll seeking attention. But the tweet is representative – there are many such comments, and some people genuinely hold such views. (Charges against Greenwood were dropped in 2023, but our point is about the way fans instinctively flocked to defend him.)

Fans support Deshaun Watson, too. There are some horrendous instances, such as fans wearing t-shirts saying "Bitch give me a massage!" and a fan holding, alongside a small child, a sign saying "Fuck them hoes/Free Watson".[4] These examples are disgusting and egregious cases, but we find more mild-mannered support, too. Robyn Lockner – a prominent fan who runs a Facebook group for women Browns fans – decided that she would make her own judgment on whether Watson was guilty, so she read a deposition from a detective and concluded that although there were two or three viable allegations, most of the women who had made allegations "just wanted money".[5] She thinks that now Watson has been suspended for 11 games, we need to move on. Lockner is clearly supporting Watson, and she is doing so vocally – these aren't just her private thoughts; she's sharing them in interviews. It's left unclear what number of serious allegations is enough for her. Would four be sufficient for her to no longer support Watson? Would she have to believe every one of the 20 or more allegations for her to think his place on the team she loves is a problem?

It's important to emphasize why supporting wrongdoers is tempting. Fans love many of their team's players, so when there is a serious objection to this adoration, rather than revising their view, they double down. Of course, ceasing to admire a player you love is often challenging: while it's hard to stop supporting somebody, it's even harder to face a threat to your identity. (This is a less powerful incentive when it comes to purists, but we'll see some problems for them later.) Although it's easy enough to say that fans shouldn't do this, an analogy with other forms of love should make clear why this isn't always easy to avoid. After all, if your spouse was credibly accused of something, would you condemn them? Maybe, but you might also find that a real struggle – after all, you love this person, and this love shapes your life in important ways – and you might find it much easier to back them and to publicly defend their reputation. This isn't to say you should back them, but we can understand why you'd do that.

It's also worth noting that the degree of this support can vary. Fans like the Mason Greenwood fan we encountered at the start of this chapter vociferously support him. Other times, this support can be a little more subtle. We might encounter purists who think that we should ignore Lionel Messi's tax issues because he is such a rare talent that we should just appreciate his soccer skills. At the weakest limit, we might even be concerned just with fans who appreciate or cheer on players.[6]

Though it's clear that much of this fan behavior is wrong, we want to point out two specific reasons why it is a problem. For one, it can protect the person accused of wrongdoing. At its worst, this can help a wrongdoer get away with what they have done, and it can help them to continue doing bad things. But it can also simply help them avoid the social censure they deserve: if a throng of fans are drowning out criticism, if players are being adored when they should be condemned, they might not learn their lessons or repent in the appropriate way.

The second issue is that this support sends a message to victims (as well as to society more broadly). It tells them that for these fans, it doesn't matter that they were, for example, raped. What matters to those fans is that this is a great player, or for partisans, this is a player for *their team*, and that matters far more to them than condemning the wrongdoing that victims have suffered.

To emphasize this second point, as Robyn Lockner herself pointed out in another interview, the signing of Deshaun Watson sent a message to women that they didn't matter.[7] The Browns were "smacking [their] female fans in the face".[8] (These interviews were published before the one in which Lockner said many of the allegations against Watson were malicious. Perhaps it became too tempting to support Watson rather than stick to her earlier moral criticism and confront the decisions the Browns made.)

There is, of course, plenty more to say here, and we won't be able to cover every issue raised by cases like this. But we'll look at how the support of fans can enable wrongdoing to continue when we turn to sportswashing; we'll explore how fans – perhaps for a good reason – perpetuate the racism inherent in the name of their teams; and along the way, we'll see what sort of message this can send to the victims of wrongdoing. But before that, we want to look at how critical fans might avoid the pitfalls of support that we have set out here.

6.1.2 Critical fans and avoiding support

Fans of immoral players, clubs, or sports face a choice: they can abandon their fandom, modify it, or end up supporting somebody or something they should not be supporting. After all, even though it is often positively good to be a sports fan, we saw in the last chapter that sometimes it isn't worth the moral costs.

In Chapter 5, we mentioned how fans of Raith Rovers responded to their team signing David Goodwillie, withdrawing their support until the club said they would no longer play him. The fans and others associated with the club showed that though they obviously valued the club (to be the women's team captain or to spend your own money sponsoring requires considerable commitment), it was not worth it to be associated with Goodwillie. Their abandonment did the opposite of what supporting him would have done: these fans made it clear that they were not prepared to condone or downplay the significance of his actions. The Raith Rovers fans effectively condemned both Goodwillie's behavior and their club for signing him. (Helping the wrongdoer get away with it is less of an issue in this case. We'll explore it more when we look at responses to sportswashing.)

By threatening to withdraw their support, the fans managed to get the change they desired. So, they could go back to being fans. Fandom matters to many of us, but it also matters to most of us that we are good people who make the right moral choices − that we do not support bad things. This was a case of *effective* abandonment. Fans got to continue cheering for their team without supporting Goodwillie's actions; they could continue to support their team without sending the message that they were OK with rape. Yet had it not been effective, the fans would have faced a major loss − either losing their fandom or crawling back to support the club despite their moral misgivings. After all, in this case, the fans thought the club had also done something wrong in signing Goodwillie. Even if fans could have avoided supporting the player, they would have been supporting the club.

Which way to go is often a very personal decision, and costs must be weighed up. But the essential thing to remember is that although being a fan is more than OK, sometimes it's better to give up fandom and all that comes with it than to support a club that signs someone like Deshaun Watson or David Goodwillie.

It's also worth remembering that even if abandonment is too hard, or too extreme, there are other options. This is the same when it comes to critical friendship. Sometimes our friends might do bad things, but we can't find it in ourselves to abandon them even if we think we should. Yet, we might still want to criticize them. Other times, they might do something that doesn't deserve abandonment, but they still deserve some censure. So, too, when it comes to fandom. How can critical fans continue to support their team if the team or a player does something awful? After all, being a fan is deeply valuable for many of us, so just abandoning fandom shouldn't be the first step.

One option is to take a step short of abandonment and instead distance yourself from your team. After Spanish club Celta Vigo signed Santi Mina, who had been accused (and has since been convicted) of sexual assault, Celta fan Sabela Correa said:

> I have to say that I did become more distant from the team, although I remained a Celta fan … Most people just said they would wait until the trial was over. I didn't like that, I would not have signed him, but I kept supporting the team, I still do. When they announced his name in the stadium, I did not applaud. But I remained a socia [club member].[9]

Correa is still a fan, but her fandom is less fervent. She still supports the club, but she cannot support Mina. By explicitly not supporting him, she makes sure she avoids sending the message that she is OK with his behavior. Rather, making a stand and refusing to applaud him sends the opposite message.

Other times, fans don't distance themselves from the team; they make explicit protests. In 2017, fans of Spanish soccer side Rayo Vallecano protested against the signing of Roman Zozulya, alleging that he was a Nazi sympathizer. The club has a left-wing ethos, and their protest (which was effective and led to Zozulya leaving the club) stemmed from this ethos. Rather than transforming their fandom and distancing themselves from their club, we can see this more as standing firm: they transformed how they engaged because they couldn't just get on with watching their team play; they had to do something. But this protest stemmed from an underlying commitment to acting in line with the ethos of their club. One might say that the team was at risk of distancing itself from its own ethos, and the fans ensured this didn't happen.

There are other forms of protest, too, which might be less direct. Since Watson signed for the Browns, there has been an increase in donations to rape crisis centers; many donations were of $22 − a symbolic amount that represents the 22 women who originally accused Watson.[10] These donations won't all be by Browns fans, but some fans will have joined this protest-by-giving. By doing this, these fans signal that they do not support Watson's behavior. Not only do they simply refuse to support him, but they actively signal that they condemn his behavior. The Browns fans who have torn up their season tickets do a similar thing, making it explicitly clear that they think his behavior is wrong, so they do not join the crowds who encourage him, or help him avoid social censure, or signal to (especially) women that they are on the side of the powerful player rather than his victims.

Even though supporting players who have done bad things is troubling, we can see that there are ways out of this. Critical fans can avoid helping wrongdoers, and they can avoid signaling that they do not care about victims. In fact, they can do precisely the opposite: they can show that they do care about this wrongdoing, and they can show that they love their team, not the wrongdoer.

6.1.3 Sportswashing

Another area where fans are – now, more than ever – embroiled in supporting wrongdoing is when club owners do wrong. This can simply involve personal wrongdoing (for example, the owner is accused of sexual assault). But what we have in mind here is something bigger: sportswashing. This is a serious topic that has rightly made its way into recent news reports and is worth exploring as a case where fans support the wrongdoing and – as we'll discuss in the final chapter – are themselves wronged by it.

So what is sportswashing? We (along with Kyle Fruh) have argued that sportswashing is when a state buys a sports club, or hosts or sponsors a competition, in order to distract from some serious wrongdoing it has been part of.[11] For instance, Saudi Arabia bought Newcastle United and is investing in LIV Golf to distract from a terrible track record on human rights, including the assassination and dismemberment of the journalist Jamal Khashoggi.[12] The UAE owns Manchester City; Qatar hosted the 2022 men's soccer World Cup and owns French giants Paris Saint-Germain. Both nations have been accused of political wrongdoing. Qatar has been accused of violating the rights of migrant workers and of discriminating against women and LGBTQ+ people.[13] The UAE, as well as detaining Matthew Hedges (whom we talked about at the end of Chapter 4), has a record of arbitrary and inhumane detention and of limiting free expression.[14] Owning their clubs and hosting the World Cup are widely regarded as attempts to wash out these sins by cleansing their moral reputations. It's important to note, however, that this isn't solely a recent thing that concerns Gulf nations investing in sports. Mussolini's Italy hosted the World Cup; Hitler's Germany hosted the Olympics. These are both seen as attempts to normalize their political wrongdoing and become accepted on the world stage.

So, how are fans involved? One important way that sportswashing works is by winning hearts and minds. There's more to be said here, but the basic idea is something we've touched on a few times already: if you like somebody, it's pretty tempting to overlook their faults. So, if a state invests a bunch of money into giving you an entertaining product to watch, or if they lead your club to success, you're going to like them. Our concern is that you are going to ignore, or even deny, the existence of, their faults. That is what the sportswasher hopes for.

If it works, then golf fans will think that the LIV tour is great, and they'll naturally start to like the owners. A vocal number of Newcastle United fans are deeply content with their new owners – owners who have invested and helped the club to become far more competitive. One fan echoed a sentiment shared by many fans when it put out a statement saying that "our football club is in the hands of people striving to make our football club the best it can be".[15] This is, at best, naive.

When fans, whether they are purist fans of golf or partisan fans of a club like Newcastle United, support these endeavors, they risk helping to enable this wrongdoing. Fans may not be on the ground committing human rights abuses, but they are helping the *sportswashing project* succeed. They do this partly just through liking the owners – after all, fans are people too, and convincing fans to overlook these faults means the sportswashers have already partly succeeded. If Newcastle fans now want Saudi Arabia to have a more prominent role on the world stage, that's a win for sportswashers. This is compounded when fans try to spread the "good" word. We saw this in Chapter 4 with the case of the UAE arresting a British PhD student on seemingly spurious charges. Though this was met with widespread condemnation, several Manchester City fans said they agreed with what the UAE had done. Why? Well, because the UAE owns Manchester City – and its investments have made City into one of the most successful clubs in the world. These fans are now on the UAE's side and are defending its political wrongdoing.

Take also the case when a section of Chelsea fans cheered for their (then) owner Roman Abramovich – who has ties to the Russian regime – during a moment of silence for victims of the war in Ukraine. These fans made it clear that they thought Abramovich was a great man, someone who deserves to be cheered and praised. If his aim in buying Chelsea was to launder his reputation, these fans certainly helped.

It's also clear that these fans sent a message: they felt it was more important to cheer for their owner than to pay respect to the victims of Russian aggression in Ukraine. When Newcastle fans cheer for their owners, they signal that it matters more to them that these people are investing in their club than the fact that these same people are key players in a political system that dismembered a dissident journalist. It sends the message that these victims don't matter.

When it comes to sportswashing, sending this message *also* helps the wrongdoer get away with the wrongdoing. If enough fans are on board, then they'll send the message that this wrongdoing doesn't matter to them. This runs the risk of encouraging other people to ignore the wrongdoing. And, since the whole point of sportswashing is to minimize reputational risks while continuing to engage in this wrongdoing, the sportswasher will have won with the help of these fans.

What can fans do about this? Some fans have abandoned their club. For instance, Newcastle fan Daniel Rey decided that he could no longer support his team and run the risk of falling for the sportswashing ploy.[16] But what about fans who don't want to abandon their club but still want to resist supporting sportswashers?

The important point to make is that supporting your club – being a fan – doesn't mean you are supporting the owners' wrongdoing or their sportswashing project. But it can be easy to fall into the trap, since it's so easy to start to like people who bring good times to your club. What seems to be key is finding a way to support your team while keeping your view of the owner distinct from this. And we have seen that this is possible, though our example doesn't come from sportswashing but from another way that fans have protested against their owners.

Some Manchester United fans, upset at how the club is owned and run by the Glazer family, have spent years wearing green and gold to matches, demonstrating that they love the club but hate the Glazers.[17] These colors are the original club colors, and by wearing them, the supporters hark back to the club's history before greed and money got involved. As they see it, the Glazers are corrupting something they love (an idea we will return to in the last chapter).[18] The Glazers are rich, and perhaps they are egoists, but they aren't engaged in sportswashing, nor have they, as far as anyone knows, committed human rights abuses that they want to cover up. Still, fans think the owners are doing something bad with their club; they are eroding the culture of a historic club. By wearing these scarves and dressing in these colors, these fans make clear that they support Manchester United, not the Glazers.

This sort of protest could inspire protests against sportswashing, too. If we want to make it clear that we do not support sportswashing – that we do not want it to succeed – and that we are not in favor of, say, human rights abuses, we can make it explicitly clear what exactly it is that we love. We love our club, or we love golf, or we love the World Cup. But we hate those who are trying to use the things that we love to get away with their own misdeeds. Fans of sportswashed clubs might want to take an example from these Manchester United fans and make it clear that though they love their club, they don't love the human rights abusers who are attempting to stuff their mouths with gold.

6.1.4 Racist names

The final example of support we had in mind concerns racist team names.

Just like the tomahawk chop that we discussed in the last chapter, we think that names like football's Kansas City (or rugby's Exeter) "Chiefs" and baseball's Atlanta "Braves" involve caricaturing and demeaning Native Americans.[19] But fans often support the use of these names. One Chiefs fan, Greg O'Neal, "slumps in his chair, looks crestfallen" when an NPR interviewer mentions changing their name; Joe Posnanski, in the same interview, was described as thinking that changing the name of his team, the Braves, was "almost unthinkable".[20] (It's worth adding that both fans – to their credit – now accept the names do need to change.)

Though this is a little speculative, we think that one reason why these names haven't been changed is that fans are so clearly attached to these names, and this helps to perpetuate the wrongdoing. By being attached to their team names, fans signal that it is more important to them that they can continue to cheer for the "Chiefs" than it is that Native Americans are treated with respect.

But this issue isn't quite as simple as it sometimes looks. We think it's worth taking a little detour here into the very identity of a team before seeing how that affects how critical fans should react. (Not to spoil things, but we are going to use some of the philosophy behind this in the concluding chapter.) We think that the fans being attached to their team's name makes some sense and carries some weight; a name is important, so we shouldn't just change it on a whim. But it isn't as important as some fans seem to think, and we should carefully (and perhaps gradually) change these names. Let us explain.

The starting point is that sports teams change. People change, too, but it's obvious (unless we get into areas of philosophy that we really don't need to get into) that Roger Federer is the same person he was 20 years ago, even though his tennis game, as well as a bunch of other aspects of his life, has changed dramatically. But what makes a sports team the same team as it was in the past?

Getting an answer to this is important, because supporting a team means supporting it over time – and partisans had better hope that they are supporting the same team from one day to the next.[21] This problem first came up in the philosophy of sport literature through a brilliant article by Stephen Mumford.

Teams go on hiatus (due to financial issues, due to war), they move stadiums or cities, they change names, their coaches and playing staff change regularly. Sometimes, this means the team no longer exists – like when they permanently fold. Sometimes, they undergo a change, yet they're clearly the same team. When Arsenal Football club moved a few hundred yards from Highbury Stadium to The Emirates Stadium, it is clear that it was Arsenal that moved. They had not died and been replaced by a new team. The same is true with the New York Mets and their move to Citi Field, which is right next to their previous ground, Shea Stadium. Other times, a team undergoes a change, and it isn't clear whether it's still the same team or not: a team might go on hiatus and then two new teams arise, each claiming the old lineage.

One example that Mumford uses is Wimbledon FC, whom we'll return to later. Wimbledon was relocated by new owners to Milton Keynes, around 50 miles away – by British standards, this is quite a distance, and certainly not just a local move – and soon took on the new name MK Dons. Fans objected that they were losing their club, and so they set up a rival club, AFC Wimbledon. Mumford asks which of these clubs, MK Dons or AFC Wimbledon, is the same as the old Wimbledon FC.

Mumford has an interesting answer about how we determine which club is the same as the original Wimbledon FC: it depends on what the fans decide. Virtually all fans continued to support Arsenal when they moved stadium; that's why it wasn't controversial whether this was a new club. But when it comes to Wimbledon, there is no clear answer: some fans think MK Dons is the same club as Wimbledon FC, while others think it's AFC Wimbledon that is the true heir.

So, what does this have to do with racist names? Whether fans think their club persists or has been replaced by something new will depend on lots of features of that club, features that help bring fans together and give them something to support.[22] Roger Federer might wear certain colors out of his personal preference or for branding reasons, but teams have team colors. Manchester United play in red; City play in blue. Their names, too, are an important part of what helps fans decide that this is still their team. The worry is that changing their name from, say, the "Chiefs" to something else is a threat to the existence of that same team, just as some fans felt that changing their team to MK Dons destroyed the club that existed before and replaced it with something else entirely.

So, we can see why there might be some resistance to changing names. If changing the name might be a threat to the existence of your team, you have reason to be wary. To some extent, this justifies why fans are so often opposed to changing their team names – but this very opposition constitutes support for wrongdoings. We think this argument only goes so far. For one, it certainly doesn't protect elements that aren't really to do with the identity of the team – like the tomahawk chop. It seems clear to us that this is racist, and although it is a fan practice many engage with, it could easily be dropped without really affecting the fan culture or the team's identity. Just beat the drum in a different way and get rid of the ridiculous chopping motion.

Also, we aren't talking about moving the Kansas City Chiefs to London; we're talking about changing the last part of their name. There are many factors that make up a team's identity, and some are much more important than others. Critical fans can ensure that the team they love persists by making sure the other parts of the team remain the same. Changing the playing staff, moving to a new city, and changing the name at the same time might affect the identity of the team, but as long as most of this remains the same, just a name change should be no great threat. As we said, the fact that Manchester United play in red and are called Manchester United is important to who they are – but they used to be called Newton Heath and as we saw earlier, would play in green and gold. A club's colors or name are important parts of them being that team, but they aren't *necessary* parts and can certainly be changed if enough elements remain the same. To put it another way: changing the name of the "Chiefs" to something else isn't like what happened to MK Dons. After all, the most important thing that happened there was that the club was moved, from Wimbledon to Milton Keynes: it's *that*, not the name change, that really made fans think it was no longer their club.

Critical fans would do better to stop supporting these names. Their support helps this wrongdoing continue, and they send a message that they don't care about this racism. Instead, they should make sure that the ownership continues to respect the other features that they love about the team. Fans can also lobby the club to make sure the new name respects the club's heritage, making the change less of a shock. For instance, The Cleveland Guardians (née Indians) are named after the Guardians of Traffic statues that stand at the ends of Cleveland's Hope Memorial Bridge. In this way, fans can safeguard the identity of their club, and they can move on from that name while recognizing the significance a name can have.

And it's worth noting that the sky has not fallen in. The Guardians and the Washington Commanders (née Redskins) have recently undergone name changes, and many fans were originally resistant, yet there has been no mass exodus of fans who think that they're no longer cheering for their team. They just don't have to cheer for a racist team name any more! The importance of a name to a team's identity shouldn't be understated, but we also shouldn't overstate it. In sports, things change, and sometimes they should change. Fans who resist name changes help to support this racism, even if this is for the non-racist reason that they worry their club's identity is under threat. But this worry is misplaced; fans can drop their resistance to a name change, keep their club, and stop perpetuating racism and signaling disdain for Native Americans.

6.2 COMPLICITY

6.2.1 What is complicity?

We now want to move on to times when fans are complicit in wrongdoing. There are many ways to be complicit. In *Death in Brunswick*, when Dave helped get rid of Mustafa's body, he became complicit in the murder. The complicity we are looking at is more insidious than this. Dave made a choice to help Carl do something illegal. We are going to look at cases where fans don't make any such choices; they are complicit just through being ordinary fans.

To do this, we want to look first at sexism and then at the exploitation of athletes. What makes these two cases troubling for a wide range of fans is that they don't involve supporting a particular club or a particular competition; rather, they can pervade entire sports, so even the purist is at risk. For instance, we will talk about exploitation and chronic traumatic encephalopathy (CTE), a traumatic brain injury that can lead to early onset dementia. Many NFL players will suffer from CTE.[23] There is also increasing evidence of a link between heading in soccer and dementia – so this is not just confined to more violent sports.[24] The same source notes that there may be a link between CTE and sports including rugby, ice hockey, lacrosse, MMA, wrestling, and boxing. The concern here is that just being a fan of one of these sports could mean you are doing something morally wrong. The same is true of the sexism that pervades many sports.

6.2.2 Sexism

Fans of many sports are, just through being ordinary fans of those sports, complicit in sexism. What we mean here is not fans gatekeeping other fans or abusing them; rather, we have in mind something that pervades the whole system of watching sports in many places: women's teams are less watched and receive far lower investments. To take one striking example, even though women's soccer is increasingly popular in the UK, and more than 17 million tuned in to watch England beat Germany in the final of Euro 2022, that pales into insignificance when compared with the almost 31 million people watching the England men's team lose in their final.[25]

The US women's national team recently reached a historic agreement that means they will be paid equally to the men's team for international matches. Not only will their pay be equal, but they will play in equally good venues and be given equally good places in which to train.[26] This wasn't handed to them by administrators desperate to create a fair world: it took a lawsuit. Nor will this equalize the massive financial disparities between the men's and women's games. Men, especially if they end up on a squad for one of the wealthy teams abroad, are often paid significantly more by their clubs, whereas the national team is the primary source of income for many of the women players.[27]

Our focus here will be on just one part of this sexism. After all, this book is about *fans*, so we won't be getting into how governments or sporting bodies should better support women's sports. And we will focus on one specific way fans can be complicit. We won't discuss, for instance, how the way that some commentators, and fans, talk about female athletes is often demeaning; the language used often focuses "disproportionately on aesthetics and personal lives".[28] Fans can clearly be complicit here. Nor will we talk about how, in some sports, like volleyball and handball, sporting associations insist that women wear form-fitting, or bikini, outfits. This isn't for any sporting reason, and it contributes to body image issues and sexualization. Though this implicates fans, it's probably a less direct issue than the issue we want to talk about.[29]

Our focus is this. How should fans respond to their sport not supporting women's teams? How should fans respond to their club not having a women's side (Manchester United, one of the world's biggest soccer teams, only recently developed a women's side)? Should fans just watch more women's sports?

Perhaps the first question here, though, is this: is there *anything* fans need to do to combat this sexism? You might think "no", and some of our arguments earlier in this book might bolster that complacency. After all, we argued that the fan communities that exist are part of the explanation for why being a fan is worthwhile. And you might think that given the fan communities around women's sports are less widespread (though certainly growing), there's not as much value in watching women's sports as there is with engaging in the bigger, more robust communities around men's sports.

But to buy into that argument would be a mistake. Firstly, the fact that a fan community is small does not mean it is worthless: often, smaller communities might be tighter-knit, and the sports team might be even more tightly embedded within the fans – you aren't likely to be neighbors with a superstar, but when it comes to smaller teams, you have a reasonable enough chance of running into a player (and perhaps not recognizing them) in the supermarket. Secondly, the fact there *isn't* the support needed to encourage these fan communities around women's teams isn't an immutable fact. Things are like this *because* of over a century of sporting sexism and in some cases, the deliberate attempts by sporting governing bodies to destroy or hinder women's sports.

For example, women's soccer was hugely popular in England in the early 1920s. Around 150 women's teams existed in 1921, with high-profile matches attracting crowds of tens of thousands.[30] A match between Dick Kerr Ladies and St Helen

Ladies in 1920 was watched by 53,000 people, with an estimated 14,000 more people denied entry to the ground after the match had sold out.[31] Rather than encouraging this enthusiasm for the women's game, the English Football Association sought to eradicate it. In 1921, they banned their members from hosting women's soccer matches at their grounds on the basis that "[t]he game of football is quite unsuitable for females and ought not to be encouraged".[32] Other football associations made similar rulings, and women's football was explicitly discouraged by many national football associations between the 1920s and the 1970s.[33]

By ignoring women's sports, fans are complicit in this sexism. The problem isn't that fans are necessarily *actively* sexist; it's that they let a sexist system continue by being uninterested in women's sports. We are guilty of this, too: no doubt had either of us paid more attention to women's sports in the past, we would have been able to furnish more examples from those arenas, and discussed issues closer to women's sports, rather than the male-dominated examples we have used throughout the book. Jake followed the England women's team at Euro 2022, but not to the same extent he followed the England men's team – watching was inconvenient and expensive, but he happily puts up with those inconveniences and expenses to watch the men. So much the worse for him – had he been a committed fan, it would have been a highlight of his sporting life.

Fans who recognize that what they have is worthwhile should try to support fandoms around women's teams. Nobody should be forced to join new communities: many of us have too many hobbies (you might not be able to watch as much sport as you'd like if you have to finish writing a book!); but if fans are looking to pick up a new team, they should at least be open to becoming fans of women's teams. This is especially true if, say, their soccer club sets up a women's side. In fact, given the history of sexism, we might say that fans should *strongly prefer* becoming fans of women's sides: women's sport has been downtrodden for long enough, and perhaps it's time to try to redress the balance.

There are other things critical fans can do, too. As we said, Manchester United only recently created a women's team. Critical fans perhaps should have put pressure on the club to create a side. Fans of the US soccer teams might have had good reason to put pressure on their national association to treat their players equitably (before the recent court case that secured equal pay). American fans of soccer might realize that they can watch not only major league soccer (the men's soccer league), but also the national women's soccer league. And fans of the MLS who say "but the quality isn't as good!" are kidding themselves: if they were in it for quality, they wouldn't be watching the MLS!

The bad news, then, is that many of us are in fact sexist in our fandom. The good news here is that being a fan of soccer, say, doesn't condemn you to being complicit in this sexism. It's just that we need to change how we are fans. To put it another way: your ordinary, bog-standard fan of many sports is likely to unwittingly be complicit in sexism, but if they are critical fans who engage with this, they can escape this complicity by paying proper attention to women's sports. The next form of complicity we are going to look at might be even harder to escape.

6.2.3 Exploitation

Many sports exploit athletes – and fans become part of this.

Sometimes, such exploitation is financial. For example, in much of American college sports, coaches and administrators make millions of dollars a year, but players (until very recently) have been banned from even selling autographs. Yet, a hundred thousand fans will still flock to see The Ohio State University play football. This is perhaps the most egregious case of financial exploitation, but even in professional leagues, there are issues. In minor league baseball, some players receive less than the equivalent of minimum wage (which in America is astoundingly low).[34] Fans still watch the minor leaguers play, and barely a protest is seen about these wages.

Perhaps an even more pressing worry arises when athletes are exploited for their bodies. Sometimes, this is perpetuated by, say, the owners, who stand to make money. But fans get plenty out of sports, too: not just entertainment, but meaningfulness and identity. If this is extracted at great cost to the players, that should trouble fans. Fans are building important parts of their lives on these sports, but this is built on the damage the players receive – even if that isn't how the fans see things, even if the fans just think they are watching sports. The problem is that the fans benefit from these bad things happening to players.[35] (This is also true when people are simply entertained by sports: and perhaps it is even more troubling if you are involved in exploiting players not for some deep meaning but just to get your kicks.)

Take the case of CTE, which we briefly discussed earlier. Philosopher Adam Kadlac has rightly pointed out that to work out the ethics here, we need to know how many players this will affect: it makes a big difference whether it's a small minority or whether it will affect a significant number – we need to know what sort of risk players are taking.[36] And, much as we have argued there are particular sporting aesthetic values, Kadlac thinks there are values available to the people who are taking part in these sports.[37] The sheer thrill of being able to do something with your body, especially something *dangerous*, can be worth a genuine risk. The MIT mathematics PhD and former NFL player John Urschel said that he *loves* hitting people.[38] We need to respect this.

For those, like Urschel, who love hitting people hard, playing American football is going to be worth the risk of a sprained ankle or an ordinary injury. We can agree that players should be free to take this risk, but surely they should be aware of the risks they face. If not, they aren't making a free choice. If we offer you a glass of something to drink that looks like wine, and you accept it, you can't really be said to have freely chosen it if it turns out that it is in fact blood, and by accepting it, you are entering our vampire cult.

It is therefore important that players are able to make an informed choice: that they know, understand, and appreciate the risks. But there is a concern that sporting bodies hide the risks from players. The NFL has been accused of doing just this.[39] And knowing the serious risk of CTE does seem to make a difference to whether footballers are willing to continue. Just a year after Urschel affirmed his commitment to putting his body on the line to chase his thrills, he quit in the wake of a study about the risk of CTE for footballers.[40]

There isn't much fans can do about this, aside from make clear that they want to know the truth about these risks. And fans only seem to be complicit if they know or should know these risks: if they are lied to as well, then they aren't exploiting the players. It's rather as if spectators at the Colosseum in Ancient Rome were tricked into thinking the gladiatorial games were a show put on by actors rather than a fight that carried the risk of serious harm or death.

By now, many fans know there are *some* risks. And it seems that science is likely to bring further insights bearing grim news. This means that fans knowingly are watching players destroy their own minds. Fans are getting enjoyment out of watching these sports. Many fans, if our arguments in this book are correct, are forming their identities and engaging in things that help bring their lives meaning by watching these sports – sports that these fans know will cause brain damage to at least some of these players.

Perhaps, critical fans should start from the idea that we might be able to reform things so that the risks aren't so great. Of course, there will always be risks in sports, and you could never make rugby or football non-contact sports; they would be different sports entirely (like touch rugby, or flag football). Yet, it might be that we can reform these sports in some way so that the changes evolve the sport without making it into something different. After all, many sports go through changes to the rules often enough with no complaint that they're getting rid of the very nature of the sport. The thrill of tackling somebody in American football or rugby isn't that you might get a brain injury if you mess up; it's that if you fail they might get past you, and they might steamroller you while they're at it. We might be able to reduce the risk of brain injury by changing protective gear or, following an interesting suggestion in rugby, limiting the number of substitutions so that players need to be fitter and cannot become so muscular and heavy, reducing the force of collisions. This might make the game safer while keeping the physical skills and thrills.

This way, players will keep their thrills, and fans will be able to watch without exploiting the players, without getting their thrills through things that bring an unnecessary risk of brain damage.[41] This is even more feasible in sports where major collisions are not central. For instance, there have been proposals to remove heading from soccer outside of the penalty box. That would still allow for headers that score goals or make impressive clearances, while removing them in the middle of the pitch in a way that doesn't really detract from the excitement of the game.

It should seem obvious, then, what a critical fan should do: press for safer measures. Rather than enjoying the game as they have always done, critical fans need to transform their participation so that they actively try to make things better. There might be limits to what they can do, but they could make their displeasure obvious and make it clear that they want to make reasonable reforms that keep the joys of physical sports while minimizing risks to players. Fans might even act like Sabela Correa refusing to applaud Santi Mina – they might love football and applaud so many of its aspects while refusing to bay and holler at the big hits. Trying to keep players safe while allowing them to enjoy their sports isn't exploitative, but cheering at unnecessarily risky collisions that might give somebody dementia is.

Yet fans only have limited power here. Unfortunately, it seems to us that in the case of CTE, fans need to keep abandonment on the table. This could be tactical abandonment to force change, or permanent abandonment if that change doesn't come about. Currently, we seem to be in an era where organizers, fans, and players are starting to better understand the scope of the risks players face. We currently know there is a risk of CTE, but perhaps the risk is low enough that we think players can freely choose to play as long as they are fully informed. But it might turn out that they are in reality at too much risk, that the only reason they continue for the sake of their livelihoods, or they are forced to continue by massive social pressure, including the expectations of fans. If the latter is the case, and there aren't appropriate moves to make sports

Why It's OK to Be a Sports Fan

safer, fans need to ask themselves whether they can continue to watch players potentially ruin their brains. It seems to us that at some point soon, fans might have to stop watching, or they'll be one step away from the exploiters who watch snuff films.[42]

6.3 CONCLUSION

We have explored how fans ought to react when the team or athlete that they love does wrong. There are many issues we have not discussed. From sports using racial stereotypes in deciding how much compensation to pay players for CTE, to teams allegedly using their private planes to help enforce draconian immigration regimes, there are too many moral issues that should concern fans.[43] There are also many ways of looking at some of these ethical topics we've discussed earlier. For instance, sportswashing might also be something that fans are complicit in. We've argued elsewhere that fans are complicit in the destruction of their sport just by being fans of sportswashed clubs or (and this is a concern for purists) competitions like LIV Golf or the World Cup.[44] We'll say a bit more about sportswashing in the final chapter, but we just wanted to flag here that the earlier discussion doesn't aim to cover all the ethical elements even for the topics we've discussed.

What should be clear is that there are plenty of ethical issues that implicate fans, and these will keep arising. Our aim has been to show some of the reasons why these issues are problems for fans and to suggest that fans can do something to fight back. They can be critical fans.

Much as there might be many ways someone can be a stylish, or powerful, or dedicated player, there are a variety of ways we might be critical fans. We all have to find our own way of dealing with the particular problems we face. How we face those problems will depend as much on what is wrong with our team, player, or sport as it will depend on what sort of person we are. A moral hardliner might go one way; someone who thinks morality is important but allows more leeway might go in another direction. Someone who is bold and confrontational might speak up or actively lead a protest; someone who is more timid might prefer subtle conversations with fellow fans. Our aim has just been to sketch the idea of a critical fan, not to explore all the ways you might be one.

What should be clear is that fans sometimes must take action; otherwise, they end up supporting a person or a club who should not be supported, or they end up complicit in things like sexism and exploitation.

But this chapter doesn't have to end on an entirely negative note. Fandom is joyous; we shouldn't be looking for moral issues everywhere, all the time. After all, personal relationships come with plenty of moral peril, too, and relationships would be *terrible* if we were always looking for moral threats. Instead, we need to be aware and conscientious, and we need to appreciate that we might have to change how we are fans, or even abandon our fandom, in response to some of the threats that do arise. We hope that the last two chapters have offered some idea of how fans can do that, so that they do not end up being fans when it is not OK to be a fan.

Conclusion: Corruption, love, and loss

We have seen in myriad ways why sometimes it isn't OK to be a sports fan, because being a fan can put you at moral risk. Being influenced by fellow fans can warp your moral views and prompt you to say or do awful things – like Clive O'Connell, the Chelsea fan who lost his job for calling Liverpool fans scum. Your favorite player might do something awful, yet your love for him means you end up supporting him – sending the message that you don't care about or believe, say, the victims of domestic violence. Your sport might be shot through with sexism, meaning that you are in danger of becoming part of the problem.

These are some of the risks of being a fan. We want to end by thinking about one final way that sports, clubs, players, and fans can be linked by wrongdoing: the fans can themselves be the victims of these wrongs. Being in love makes you vulnerable – your partner might leave you, they might cheat, or they might let you down. The same is true for sports teams. And when your team or sport wrongs you, just as with romantic love, this can cut deep, because being a fan is part of what makes you who you are and gives meaning to your life.

What do we have in mind here? We are going to focus on two forms of this that are both based on the bad behavior of owners. The first is sportswashing, the second when owners move a club to a new city. Both of these are based on the bad

DOI: 10.4324/9781003271277-8

behavior of owners. But it is worth pausing to make clear that so many of the issues we discussed in Chapter 6 also wrong the fans. When players do something awful, they put the moral records of their fans on the line; likewise, when sporting bodies continue to exploit players, they put fans in a position where they can only enjoy their sport through this exploitation. At a certain point, critical fans are forced to consider whether the team or the sport they love is worth the fandom, and uncritical fans get swept up in ignorant wrongdoing. Forcing this on fans is a way of wronging them, too.

7.1 SPORTSWASHING, AGAIN

We have already discussed how sportswashing can make fans complicit in wrongdoing. But that is not all that is wrong with it. Sportswashing wrongs fans in the same way I wrong you if I destroy something you love. Well, not just something you love, but something that is important to who you are. Sportswashing takes something that shapes people's identities and gives meaning to their lives and uses it to wash the blood from the reputations of the rich and powerful. Whereas before, you might have been able to watch the World Cup or the golf and just enjoyed the spectacle, now you're watching what you know is an effort to get people to forget about human rights abuses. Whereas before you could cheer for your club (even if it is one that wrings money out of you in the service of greedy, egomaniacal owners), you now can only cheer for blood money.

In the most extreme cases, sportswashing is roughly akin to someone taking over the house you grew up in, the house your great-grandparents built with their own hands, and turning it into a Nazi shrine. It takes something you cherished and makes it filthy. For purists, it's roughly akin to taking a painting you loved and defacing it. Not all cases will be quite so extreme, but we hope this gets our point across. And the sad fact is that often there is very little that fans can do about sportswashing.

Sure, fans can resist. They might protest, accepting that they love their club while continuing to despise their owners. They might do something like the Manchester United fans with their green and gold scarves that indicate their loyalty to the traditions of the club and disavowal of the owners. But entire fandoms often enough get behind sportswashing and welcome the money coming to their club or sport. That is part of what makes sportswashing so destructive: it co-opts fans into the unwitting moral destruction of the thing that they love.

Critical fans often find themselves in a difficult minority. Though fans might try to fight it, in many cases, they may worry that the only acceptable approach will be to abandon their fandom and refuse to blot their moral record by supporting a club financed by human rights abusers – abusers who are supported by a majority of the rest of the fanbase.

It is also worth making a broader point. We are often not wary enough about how much power these people can have over the fans. Sporting authorities have let us down by allowing Qatar to host the World Cup, and by allowing Saudi Arabia to own Newcastle United. But until enough fans make a noise about it, they'll be at risk of being part of the next great sportswashing project, too. Critical fans need to be proactive, because once sportswashing gets started, it can be very hard to resist.

7.2 UPROOTED

Though the futility of critical fandom is particularly stark when it comes to sportswashing, in one way, this is the same with many of the moral issues we have discussed already: critical fans can try to change how they engage with their team, they can try to force the club to improve, but sometimes, it becomes clear that no good can come from this resistance. At some point, either fans will be forced into engaging in fandom in a way that is not OK, in a way that leads them into wrongdoing, or they will be forced into abandonment.

Critical fans are sometimes forced into making this choice between bad fandom and abandonment. But things are even starker for fans whose club is entirely removed. Those fans aren't even given a choice of what to do, since they are abandoned by their club. To see this, it's worth looking at some less extreme cases of owners messing around with things that might be important to fans.[1]

We saw in Chapter 6, when we were discussing team names, that several different features help to make a sports club into the thing that fans love, and these features help to keep it the same club over time. Owners can fiddle with these features, ranging from the small, identity-denting, to the major, identity-disrupting sort of change. A few years ago, the chairman of Cardiff City Football Club decided to change their blue kit to a red kit, because he thought red was a luckier color. But that was the only change. Nobody could seriously deny that this was Cardiff, though they might think that Cardiff should play in blue. Other times, fans are just going to be upset at the direction the club is going in – like the Manchester United fans who wave green and gold scarves as a protest against the club's owners. That might be frustrating, but we are going to end by focusing on things that are much worse than merely irritating.

At other times, the changes are more drastic. European sports fans are creeped out by the American practice of moving teams around the country. It might not happen quite as regularly as Europeans imagine, but big teams move often enough. The Baltimore Colts upped and left for Indianapolis in the middle of the night. Moves happen in the UK, too, as we saw with Wimbledon FC becoming (officially, though not in the eyes of AFC Wimbledon fans) MK Dons. Although sometimes it won't be clear if this is the same team, what should be clear is that *sometimes* the team will have been destroyed, and even if that doesn't happen, the team has been uprooted, and the fans are left in a sort of limbo. Their team is still playing, and they can follow on the TV. For some fans, this won't make any difference: if you already live hundreds or thousands of miles away, the stadium your team plays in might not matter. But it can be devastating to local fans.

After all, if you spend your Saturday morning getting breakfast with your friends, then walk down to the pub for a pre-game pint and take your place in the seat you've sat in to watch your team for decades – and were joined in this in earlier years by your grandfather, who similarly had been there for decades – having that tradition taken away is massive. Something that lent meaning to the lives of fans, something that shaped their identities, has been wrenched from them. By uprooting a team, by plonking it down in a new place where it has no history, owners don't just leave the team rootless; they leave fans rootless, too.

When clubs do *break* their identity, critical fans are left with no choice but to decide whether to abandon or criticize their team. They can't abandon their team; their team has abandoned them – killed off by uncaring owners.

Perhaps sometimes, they could take some other steps. They might follow the new team. Although MK Dons are not Wimbledon, fans might think that *something* persists that enables them to build up something to replace what they have lost: it may be that fellow fans have followed the club or that historic figures from the club's glory days have shifted to the new club. It won't be the same, but it might still be worthwhile. This is a bit like being invested in a romantic relationship, and stung by the fact your then-partner has fallen out of romantic love with you, you persist in friendship (when what you really wanted was for the romance to continue).

Or, abandoned fans might start something new. That's what fans of Wimbledon did when they created AFC Wimbledon. By doing this, they obviously aren't continuing with Wimbledon exactly as it was, since the trophy cabinet and league placement were dragged off to Milton Keynes. Instead, what they are doing is trying to create something to replace it, but to replace it in a more faithful way than they think the owners are doing up in Milton Keynes.

No doubt, there is something depressing about having to take either of these steps, and we should see that plenty is lost whether you support the relocated team or create a new one. But fans have even fewer options elsewhere. The English soccer league structure is huge. There are 92 league teams, and below that, hundreds of semi-professional or amateur teams. The NFL has only 32 teams. There is no robust lower-league system. (The college system is comparable to the English soccer structure but is nevertheless very different.) When the Colts left Baltimore, the city lasted a decade without a team. To get a team back, they needed an owner and for the NFL to grant them a franchise. Fans couldn't just club together and create something new. In that situation, fans are left mostly helpless. Following a team hundreds of miles away in Indiana is hardly the same as supporting your city's side.

Abandoning or trying to transform your team comes with costs – you lose your fandom, or you have to go through the effort of trying to enact real change while putting up with immorality in the thing you love. But there are upsides: you can stand by your principles, or you can reform something you love into something better, no longer tarnished by immorality. Even if you lose your fandom, you can be proud of the choice you made. But when fans are abandoned by their club, they're sometimes left with few meaningful choices at all.

7.3 LOVE AND LOSS

Destroying a club isn't necessarily the worst thing owners can do. Some of them are human rights abusers on a grand scale. Nor is it the most morally repugnant thing that happens in sport; the last chapters have contained enough violence to make that clear. But there is something perverse about how sports can bring such value to their fans, and owners can just yank this away. In a world where power and money count for a lot, we would do well to pay attention not just to how sports fans behave, but also to how they are treated.

We also need to accept that what lends meaning to our lives, and what we use to create our identities, is not fully in our control.[2] It is influenced by the ties we have with others, the communities we are part of, and grand things like war and the circumstances we face. When those close to us act badly, it often reflects badly on us. When our country invades another, it reflects badly on us. When our fellow fans are violent and sexist, it reflects badly on us. And the things we love, which lend meaning to our lives and shape who we are, can become corrupted, as when a family member does something awful.

We could try and avoid this by not forming any of these ties and not accepting any communal identities; but this is both unrealistic and undesirable. We would be characterless, boring, and our lives would be bland and uninteresting. We *must* form these connections; we *must* invest in things like fandom that lend meaning to our lives. But we also must accept that we are not fully in control, and sometimes, things can go very wrong. Sometimes, we can try to work towards improving things. You don't abandon your family just because your father did something awful; instead, you try to stop others from sliding into the same pit. Abandonment comes only when the possibility of change is hopeless.

Sometimes, though, things are taken away against our will: marriages are wrenched apart, people die, we die – often earlier than we would like. Much as we might sometimes justifiably leave our friends, they might leave us – and sometimes, they might do that for no good reason at all, driven by malice, apathy, or selfishness. Yet, none of that stops us from loving others and trying to lead a meaningful life. The same is true with fandom. As with anything worthwhile, it comes with risks, and at worst, all can turn to ashes. As fans, we need to guard firmly against our fandom or our team turning bad. We need to be critical fans. It's just that sometimes, no matter how hard we try, our fandom can be taken away from us or turned into something we can no longer support.

***

As we finished the first draft of this book, the 2022 men's soccer World Cup had just ended. As we discussed in Chapter 6, the competition was held in Qatar, a country with an appalling record of human rights abuses that used the World Cup to try to bolster its international reputation. If they are successful in this (and, even after the competition is over, it is not yet clear to us whether this attempt at sportswashing will succeed), it will be down to all of the wonderful things that make a World Cup so engrossing. The supremely talented players gracing the tournament with their skill, the beautiful goals, mazy dribbles, crunching tackles, and tactical masterclasses. It will be down to the passion of the fans as they triumph in victory or console each other in defeat. It will be down to the memorable ways in which journalists and commentators describe and analyze the games.

The World Cup is an obvious choice of tournament to use for sportswashing because of its rich and illustrious history. Many of the most memorable moments in soccer history have taken place at World Cups: from Brazil's fantastic team goal finished by Carlos Alberto in 1970, to Maradona's incredible dribbled goal from his own half in 1986 (followed shortly after by his infamous "Hand of God" goal), to Senegal's unbelievable opening-day win against defending champions France in 2002. This World Cup was no different, with Morocco's incredible displays making them the first African team to reach the World Cup semi-finals. Sadly, all of these things that make the World Cup special and memorable have been put to the service of improving the international reputation of human rights abusers.

Despite all this, we both watched. We did, of course, feel conflicted about this, but when England faced up in their final group game against local rivals Wales (playing in their first World Cup since 1958), our eyes were glued to our televisions. When Argentina beat France in a thrilling final, and Lionel Messi (one of the world's best ever players) won the trophy for the first time, we were both watching, enraptured by the game that we both love so much.

INTRODUCTION

1. A note on "soccer": *yes*, we are using "football" to refer to American football, and "soccer" to refer to what most of the world calls "football". Are we happy with that? No! But talking about "association football" and "American football" would make us sound like Victorians or posh schoolboys and would push us over the word limit.
2. As reported in Old Firm Facts 2021.
3. Old Firm Facts 2021.
4. Old Firm Facts 2021.
5. Howard 1912, 46. Cited in Wann & James 2018, 175.
6. Cummings 2013.
7. Cited in Matthew 2014.
8. Sportssuck.org. See Wilson 2002 for an overview of the related "anti-jock movement".
9. Lasch 1979, 22.
10. Cohan 2019, 137.
11. Cohan 2019, 138.
12. Gough 2022.

1

1. Koebert 2021. This survey took in over 1,500 NFL fans with at least 20 from each team. The survey was taken between May and July 2021, and respondents were "asked to outline their spending and fandom habits during a typical NFL season, such as those prior to the COVID-19 pandemic".
2. eToro 2019.
3. Harmsen 2021.

4. Pandian 2018.

5. Cerami 2022. We won't say very much about fans of individual players (either fans of team sports who, say, idolize Lionel Messi or fans of players in individual sports like tennis), partly because we think that there are more pressing ethical issues for fans of contemporary team sports – but plenty of what we say will also apply to fans of individuals.

6. Rutherford 2020.

7. Sections 1.2–1.5 draw significantly on Archer (2021).

8. Nozick (1989, 82).

9. Dixon 2001 and Mumford 2012a also draw an analogy between fandom and love, claiming that both arise from some form of accident, have an intentional object, and persist through time. Similarly, Kadlac 2022, 58 notes the contingent nature of most sports fandom by acknowledging that if facts about his history had been different, then he would have been a fan of a different team.

10. Dixon 2001, 152.

11. Tarver 2017, 28.

12. Giulianotti 2016, 5.

13. Quinn 2009, 105.

14. Behrens and Uhrich 2020; Fazal-E-Hasan et al. 2021.

15. Jollimore 2011, 29.

16. Jollimore 2011, 29.

17. Jollimore 2011, 48.

18. Mumford 2012a, 11–12.

19. Kolodny 2003.

20. Sandvoss 2005, 104.

21. Mumford 2004; Tarver 2017; Wojtowicz 2021.

22. See Protasi 2016 for a defense of the claim that unrequited love can be just as genuine and valuable as requited love.

23. Kolodny 2003.

24. For a full defense of the idea that we can and should love non-human animals, see Rudy (2011).

25. Shpall 2018, 96.

26. Nussbaum 2013, 208.

27. We take this account of partisans from Dixon (2001).

28. Here, we follow Mumford's (2012a, 10) understanding of the difference between purists and partisans.

29. Giulianotti (2002) uses this additional distinction to identify four kinds of supporter identity. *Supporters* are those with a traditional, partisan commitment to a club, who are passionately emotionally invested in a team. *Fans* have a consumer, partisan relationship with their team and strongly identify with them despite not having a strong local or cultural connection with them. *Followers* favor teams as a result of some noneconomic identification with the team, though they are unlikely to feel passionately about that team and so are not strongly partisan. *Flâneurs* are spectators who have a detached relationship with the game and with their fellow fans. Flâneurs may follow individual teams and so count as partisans, but their commitment is likely to be weak.

2

1. Fowles 2017, 4–5.
2. Rushden 2020.
3. Fowles 2017, 4.
4. Branscombe and Wann 1991.
5. Wann et al. 2011b; Wann, Polk, and Franz 2011a.
6. Doyle et al. 2016.
7. Wann and James 2018, 184.
8. Olmsted 2021, 14.
9. Elias and Dunning 1986, 44.
10. Elias and Dunning 1986, 70.
11. Elias and Dunning 1986, 40.
12. Elias and Dunning 1986, 70.
13. Elias and Dunning 1986, 31.
14. Elias and Dunning 1986, 82.
15. Morris 2019, 163.
16. Ross 2017, 53.
17. Fowles 2017, 6.
18. Fowles 2017, 268.
19. Lanchester 2020.
20. Tarver 2017.
21. Anderson 2006, 6.
22. Kalman-Lamb 2021.
23. Dyreson 2003, 93.

24. Hobsbawm 1990, 143. Needless to say, although sports have historically been male-dominated, Hobsbawm's quote needn't be restricted to men.

25. Hornby 1992, 179.

26. For an account of the decline of religion, see Inglehart 2021. For an account of the decline in trade union membership, see Sano and Williamson 2008.

27. Crawford 2004, 62.

28. Fowles 2017, 194. A similar point is made by the sociologist Nathan Kalman-Lamb 2021, 928, who argues that becoming a fan is a response to "the atomistic alienation of neoliberal society".

29. Fowles 2017, 194.

30. Edmundson 2015.

31. As the sociologist John Williams argues in Ross 2017, 53.

32. Kwame Anthony Appiah – whom you might know as the New York Times's resident ethicist – introduces the term "ethical identity" (1990, 495). Imagine somebody born in your body, but into a different ethnicity, or raised with a different gender. On some accounts of identity, such a person would still be you, but Appiah thinks that when we think about ethical identity, such a person would not be you because their ethical identity is too different from yours.

33. Ben-Porat 2010, 280.

34. Fowles 2017, 7.

35. For more, see Cocking and Kennett 1998, 504 and Lopez-Cantero and Archer 2020.

36. Tarver 2017, 1.

37. Rubin 2015.

38. Elias and Dunning 1986, 220.

39. Wann and Fast 2021.

40. Wolf 1997, 209. Tarver also uses the term "active engagement" (2017, 25).

41. Wolf 1997, 209.

42. These are Wolf's examples (1997, 211).

43. One might hit this with a nihilistic "Nothing is meaningful! It's all a waste of time!". But if that is your response, you have bigger worries than whether it's OK to be a sports fan. We are assuming that life can

indeed be meaningful, and things can be worth doing: our task is to show that fandom can be one of those things.

44. Wolf 1997, 217.
45. Wolf 1997, 217. Wolf here is arguing against Richard Taylor's (1970) view that Sisyphus may have a meaningful life.
46. Mumford 2021, 1.
47. Mumford 2021, 2.
48. Mumford 2021, 4.
49. Mumford 2021, 4.
50. For key works on the nature of games, play, and sport, see Huizinga 2014; Nguyen 2020; Suits 2014. For introductions to the philosophy of sport, see Devine & Frias 2020 and Ryall 2016.
51. Edmundson 2015, 3–4.
52. Fowles 2017, 216.
53. Kadlac 2022, 32.
54. Kadlac 2022, 36.
55. Kadlac 2022, 37.
56. Foster Wallace 2006.
57. Kadlac 2022, 37.
58. Kadlac 2022, 37–38.
59. Foster Wallace 2006.
60. Gumbrecht 2006, 37.
61. Gumbrecht 2006, 38–39.
62. Though this does not mean that we should think that sports are arts. As David Best 1974, 212 points out, many things are beautiful without being artistic, such as sunsets, mountain ranges, and birdsong. The difference between the aesthetic and the artistic, according to Best, is that the artistic must "at least allow for the possibility of a close involvement of life situations" such as "contemporary moral, social, political and emotional issues". We will not enter into this debate, as we only wish to make the point that watching sports can be aesthetically valuable.
63. Mumford 2021, 8.
64. Edgar 2013, 117.
65. Davis 2015 argues that appreciating beauty has an important role to play in sports fandom alongside appreciation of the aesthetic features Edgar mentions.

66. Foster 2010, 255–256, referring to Wilson 2018, ch. 2 – which explores the example of how British and South American soccer evolved to favor different styles.
67. Foster 2010, 257.

3

1. Litman 2013.
2. Magee 2020.
3. This section draws on our Archer and Wojtowicz 2022.
4. NPR 2022.
5. Wildman 2019, 261. Another fictionalist, Kendall Walton, wonders why people care so much about the Red Sox or the Yankees when "[t] heir fortunes on the field have no obvious bearing on the welfare of most fans". Walton 2015, 76.
6. This is what Nils-Hennes Stear (2017, 275) calls the *puzzle of sport*. Stear offers other useful criticisms of the fictionalists.
7. For a critical take on this, see Stear 2017.
8. Borge 2019, 20.
9. Wildman, 2019, 272.
10. Walton 2015, 77–78.
11. Stear is critical of this and thinks that there are other explanations, which don't lead to the conclusion that fans care only fictionally, and that explain why our emotional investment can differ.
12. Walton 2015, 77.
13. Sid Lowe (2013) offers a detailed history of Real Madrid and Barcelona that provides far more detail on each club's ethos.
14. Wilson 2019b, 92–96.
15. Wilson 2019b, 95.
16. Tarver 2017, 2.
17. Tarver 2017, 28.
18. It's worth clarifying that while it's clear that there are communities of fans, it is also clear that there are often communities within these communities. There might be schisms and splits between different fan groups, and these groups may have different ideas about what it means to be a fan of this team. The fact remains, though, that there is a community of Indiana Fever fans, a community of Buffalo Bills fans, and a community of Partick Thistle fans.

19. A bolder claim in the philosophy of sports literature is that the community of fans is also part of the club. We may wish to be careful, though, of identifying the fans too closely with the team on the pitch. Adam Kadlac has warned against this tendency, arguing that sports fans should not say things like "We won the game"; because the fans are observers rather than participants, they make no contribution to the winning of the game (Kadlac 2022, ch. 3). We do not wish to take a stand on this issue but simply wish to emphasize that the community of fans succeeds when the club succeeds.
20. Mumford 2012a, 12.
21. Mumford 2012a, 17.
22. See Russell (2012) for a defense of the view that the different ways of watching sport are equally valuable.
23. Elliott 1974, 110.
24. Dixon 2001, 153.
25. See López Frías 2012.
26. Nicholas Dixon 2001, 153, 2016 calls this "moderate partisanship".
27. Mumford 2012b, 373.
28. See Edgar 2016 for an interesting, related discussion of the three ways of watching a sports video.
29. Paul Davis 2018 notes that sketching the partisan as being concerned only with the result seems flawed: they want to see their team excel!.
30. Kadlac 2022, 47.
31. López Frías 2012.
32. Dixon 2016, 246.
33. Adam Kadlac (2022, 54–55) makes a similar point that partisan fans help make the experience richer for purists too.

4

1. Gordon 2016.
2. Kapuściński 1986.
3. Russell 2016.
4. Russell 2016.
5. For an account of the conflict and its build up, see Chirinos 2018 and Kapuściński 1986.
6. Fox 2016.
7. Ali 2021.

8. Milekić 2016.
9. Orwell 2003, ch. 12.
10. Orwell 2003, ch. 12.
11. Orwell 2003, ch. 12.
12. Orwell 2003, ch. 12.
13. Tännsjö 1998, 25.
14. For the low, official numbers, see Cardenas 2022. For higher numbers, see Baxter 2022.
15. Baxter 2022.
16. Feezell 2013, 81. Tännsjö 1998 goes further and argues that our admiration for sporting heroes requires, as long as we are consistent, that we also feel contempt for the losers.
17. Tännsjö 1998, 24.
18. Cross 2016.
19. See Kadlac 2022 ch.4 for a discussion of the ways fans can mistreat athletes by objectifying them and failing to see them as human beings.
20. Partick Thistle 2020a.
21. Wilson 2020.
22. Partick Thistle 2020b.
23. Partick Thistle 2020c.
24. Campos 2022.
25. This argument and example are from Robshaw 2021, 2–3.
26. Keegan 2022.
27. Royals.org 1999.
28. Jolly 2011.
29. Dixon 2001.
30. See Erwin 1992; Kleinig 2022.
31. Though see Fruh et al. (2021) for a defense of fair weather fandom.
32. Aristotle (1985) *Nicomachean Ethics* Book II.1.
33. This argument is made by Russell (2012).
34. For further discussion of the arbitrariness of fandom and the fact that we would likely be fans of different teams if certain features of our history were different, see Kadlac 2022, 58.
35. At least, this is not *deeply* arbitrary – it's no more arbitrary than, say, being born into a particular religion. Though there is a sense in which these things are arbitrary, it's not arbitrary in the same way as the shallowness of turning the TV on at a particular time or moving to a particular city.

36. See Fequiere (2018) for a list of strange ways people have met their partners.
37. This argument is made by Dixon (2016).
38. It's worth adding that fans are, in a sense, also engaging in teamwork. Not only do they show that they are willing to persist; they show they are willing to work with others in a common project with shared goals. They work together so the club succeeds. Fandom could also be a great antidote to egoism: a fan has to care about more than *herself*.
39. Brady 2019, 125.
40. Brady 2019, 119.
41. Brady 2019, 125.
42. Newson et al. 2021.
43. See Whitehouse et al. 2017.
44. Crook 2019.
45. Kleinig 2022.
46. This point is made by Dixon (2001).
47. Cocking and Kennett 2000.
48. Cocking and Kennett 2000, 280.
49. Hedges 2019.
50. Wilson 2019a.

5

1. Staufenberg 2015.
2. These pose similar problems to the fan as racism, sexism, and violence do – and the critical fan can respond similarly to them – so we won't spell them out specifically.
3. There might be certain cultural differences between hooligans and ultras, and violence seems more ingrained in hooligan culture, but this is not the place for an in-depth discussion.
4. Ordinary fans are also called "Blades", as are the team. Here, we are talking about the hooligan group.
5. See especially Armstrong 1998, chs 1 and 2.
6. Jones 2019a.
7. Jones 2019b.
8. For more information on the political turmoil in Belarus and the role of sports fans in protesting it, see Beardsworth 2021 and Wilczek 2022. That said, ultras are not exactly always on the progressive side

of the political lines: for instance, in Serbia, groups of ultras have been used by the regime to quash political dissent; see Eror 2021.

9. Armstrong 1998, 29–30.
10. Jones 2016.
11. Victory 2009.
12. www.youtube.com/watch?v=IScx2xAgV4g Accessed August 28th, 2022.
13. BBC News 2012.
14. Maske 2002. It should be noted that "de-escalation" is not a concept American police are particularly familiar with; they like pepper balls in the way that Jose Mourinho likes complaining about the referee.
15. BBC News 2001.
16. https://en.wikipedia.org/wiki/List_of_violent_spectator_incidents _in_sports Accessed August 28th, 2022.
17. https://en.wikipedia.org/wiki/Nika_riots Accessed August 28th, 2022.
18. Anderson 1991. See also Bates 2013, and see Tarver 2017 for an in-depth critique of "mascotting".
19. Bonesteel and Payne 2017.
20. Hirst 2013.
21. Associated Press 2021.
22. Gary Armstrong talks about this briefly in terms of the history of soccer in Sheffield; see Armstrong 1998, 7–8.
23. Tarver 2017, 39.
24. Tarver 2017, 34.
25. Pope 2013.
26. Pope 2013, 263.
27. Tarver 2017, 174.
28. Football Supporters' Association 2021, 4.
29. Rushden 2021.
30. Armstrong 1998, 6.
31. Jones 2019b.
32. MacInnes 2021.
33. Richards 2021.
34. See Archer and Matheson 2019.
35. Cialdini et al. 1976.

36. Fair weather fans are often criticized by other fans and by philosophers of sport. See, for example, Dixon 2001, Mumford 2012a, 10, and Russell 2012; but Fruh et al. 2021 defend fair weather fandom.

37. Snyder, Lassegard, and Ford 1986.

38. Sherman 1987.

39. See Wolf 2010.

40. In this book, we are using the same notion of critical fandom that Alfred discusses in Archer 2021.

41. We introduce these two options in a paper with Kyle Fruh on sportswashing; Fruh, Archer, and Wojtowicz 2023.

42. We discuss the Goodwillie case as the sort of response a critical fan might make in Fruh, Archer, and Wojtowicz 2023. For a summary of the case, see BBC News 2017b.

43. We discuss this in Fruh, Archer, and Wojtowicz 2023.

44. Pantelick 2022.

45. Archer 2021.

46. For another example, see the LeBron James Grandmothers' Fan Club, discussed at Tarver 2017, 183–186.

47. Davis 2012, 6. Note that Davis thinks there might be wider-reaching downsides to the Ladies that we need to recognize: it might be that male fans restrain themselves not through recognizing that what they are doing is wrong, but because they are under the influence of a patriarchal mode of thought in which women are weak and cannot deal with "the vulgarities of the public world" (9) – and the Ladies end up reinforcing male hegemony through this. Exploring this claim is way beyond our scope, but Davis provides an interesting and developed line of thought.

48. Tomasetti 2015.

49. Some argue that this does in fact trade on bad stereotypes; see Christopher 2020.

50. Alfred says more about some of the difficulties of being a critical fan in Archer 2021.

51. López Frías 2012. López Frías goes on to develop an account that says we need to be virtuous people as well as fans, and this obliges us to have some moral standards when we are fans: we can be biased and committed to our own team when it comes to sports, but we need to step outside of this when other people's moral integrity is under

threat. His account is especially interesting in talking about some of the ways that sporting bodies could help to encourage better, more critical fans – something that we don't discuss in depth here.

6

1. See Archer and Matheson 2019 for a discussion of this shame. For a discussion of the idea that players have a special duty to be good role models, see Feezell 2013 ch. 6; Howe 2020; Spurgin 2012; Wellman 2003. See Yorke and Archer 2020 for an argument that sporting celebrities have special duties to act virtuously that arise from their role as ambassadors for the game.
2. Halliday 2022.
3. https://twitter.com/nani_ashaba/status/1552857595748257793?s=20 &t=tM9y2eyb7tc_UyCqTE-3Lw – tweeted 28th July, 2022, accessed 29th August, 2022. Spelling and grammar mistakes are in the original.
4. Phillips 2022.
5. Caldwell 2022.
6. Megs Gendreau thinks that when we watch sports, we are admiring *the person* who plays the sport. When we admire a painting, we might admire the end result, not the painter, but "athletic achievement is intimately linked to particular persons" (2022, 280). We might worry, then, that admiring a sportsperson who has done something wrong means that we are admiring somebody who does not deserve to be admired. But that's an issue we are going to set aside, since it brings up too many complications.
7. Hewitt 2022.
8. Morgan and Tumin 2022.
9. Corrigan 2022.
10. Caldwell 2022.
11. Fruh, Archer, and Wojtowicz 2023.
12. BBC News 2021.
13. Amnesty International 2021a.
14. Amnesty International 2021b.
15. https://twitter.com/worflags/status/1578100869169831936 October 6th, 2022, accessed October 8th, 2022.
16. Rey 2021.
17. Conn 2010.

18. Andrew Edgar (2021) has a fascinating short piece on how money corrupts sports, which we (with Kyle Fruh) discuss in more depth in Fruh, Archer, and Wojtowicz 2023.
19. For a detailed argument about the wrongness of these names, as well as a discussion of other arguments in this area, see Tarver 2017, ch. 3. Tarver's argument turns around mascots and symbols more broadly, though we focus just on names. Her argument is more complicated than we set out in the text. It builds on the fact – which we discuss later – that names (and other symbols) help to unify the team. The caricatured fearsome Indian is used to symbolize the team, and this helps create the team's identity – but only works if Native Americans are kept at a distance by fans; otherwise, the caricature loses weight. So, fans use these Native Americans, by caricaturing them, for their own purposes.
20. Greene 2020.
21. Mumford 2004, 185–186.
22. See Tarver 2017, ch. 3.
23. For an overview of how CTE affects sportspeople, and some statistics, see Galgano, Cantu, and Lawrence 2016.
24. Whitehead 2022.
25. BBC Sport 2022.
26. US Soccer 2022. See Archer and Prange 2019 for an examination of the moral arguments in favor of equal pay for men's and women's national soccer teams.
27. Carlisle 2022.
28. Fox 2021.
29. Wuertz 2021.
30. Williams 2007.
31. Tate 2013.
32. Tate 2013, 227.
33. Oosterbaan and Prange 2017.
34. Weaver 2018. There have been recent efforts to change these pay conditions, including through unionization.
35. Kadlac notes his discomfort at realizing he wouldn't let his son play football, but he is "happy to have others sacrifice their mental health for my enjoyment even as I regard my son's brain as too precious to expose to the punishment football can mete out": Kadlac 2022, 79.

36. Kadlac 2022, 78.
37. Kadlac 2022, ch. 2.
38. Rosenwald 2016.
39. Belson 2017.
40. Chiari 2017. We should also recognize that players often have a huge incentive to play even if they wouldn't freely make that choice. After all, at the top level, they have built their lives on this. They recognize a debt to themselves and others: their families have helped them, pouring in hours and hours a week, and money after money; the players themselves have trained for thousands of hours, further relying on the help of so many coaches and supporters. What's more, they often *love* the sport. The pressures on players – including pressures they put on themselves – to continue might mean that these choices are less free than they seem.
41. We say "unnecessary risk" because many sports will inherently have a risk of major injury, including brain damage – and we might think that *some* risk is an acceptable tradeoff for the benefits of playing and watching these sports. The exploitation problem is much sharper when the players are compelled to do something *too* risky.
42. Our claims here are very much in line with George Tyler's 2021 view that fans have a forward-looking collective moral responsibility to take steps to mitigate football's unacceptable risks.
43. For more on "race norming", which the NFL ended in 2021, see Canada and Carter 2021.
44. Fruh, Archer, and Wojtowicz 2023.

CONCLUSION

1. We'll leave cases where fans are just financially exploited by owners, because even though this is awful, the moral issues there are a bit less interesting.
2. Adam Kadlac (2022, 56–57) takes this point and suggests that being a fan can help us appreciate this and can imbue in us a sort of "humility and openness" that helps us deal with the waves of (mis)fortune elsewhere in life. Our point is not about what sports can teach us, it's about how the love involved in fandom is risky, like the love involved in these other things.

References

Ali, Zakariyya. "The football match that started a war". *Varsity*, 26th September 2021. Accessed 11th September 2022. Available at: https:// www.varsity.co.uk/sport/22092?fbclid=IwAR1ZZOcrSykdqQawi jTfddquj_lMt37U3gBlLicZgrcE2nvMjm7gzvMgU1Y.

Amnesty International "Qatar 2021". *Amnesty.Org*, 2021a. Accessed 12th October 2022. Available at: https://www.amnesty.org/en/location/ middle-east-and-north-africa/qatar/report-qatar/.

Amnesty International. "United Arab Emirates 2021". *Amnesty.org*, 2021b. Accessed 23rd October 2022. Available at: https://www.amnesty.org /en/location/middle-east-and-north-africa/united-arab-emirates/ report-united-arab-emirates/.

Anderson, Benedict. *Imagined Communities: Reflections on the Origin and Spread of Nationalism* (Revised Edition). London: Verso, 2006.

Anderson, Dave. "Sports of the times; The Braves' Tomahawk phenomenon". *The New York Times*, 13th October, 1991. Accessed 28th August 2022. Available at: https://www.nytimes.com/1991/10/13/sports/sports-of -the-times-the-braves-tomahawk-phenomenon.html.

Appiah, Kwame Anthony. "'But would that still be me?' Notes on gender, 'race,' ethnicity, as sources of 'identity'". *The Journal of Philosophy* 87(10) (1990): 493–499.

Archer, Alfred. "Fans, crimes and misdemeanors: Fandom and the ethics of love". *The Journal of Ethics* 25(4) (2021): 543–566.

Archer, Alfred and Benjamin Matheson. "Shame and the sports fan". *Journal of the Philosophy of Sport* 46(2) (2019): 208–223.

Archer, Alfred and Jake Wojtowicz. "It's much more important than that: against fictionalist accounts of fandom". *Journal of the Philosophy of Sport* 49(1) (2022): 83–98.

Archer, Alfred and Martine Prange. "'Equal play, equal pay': moral grounds for equal pay in football". *Journal of the Philosophy of Sport* 46(3) (2019): 416–436.

Aristotle. *Nicomachean Ethics*. Translated by T. Irwin. Indianapolis: Hackett Publishing, 1985.

Armstrong, Gary. *Football Hooligans: Knowing the Score*. New York: Berg, 1998.

Associated Press. "Kyrie Irving cites 'underlying racism' after fan arrested for throwing bottle". *The Guardian*, 31st May 2021. Accessed 28th August 2022. Available at: https://www.theguardian.com/sport/2021/may/31/kyrie-irving-fan-arrest-bottle-nba-celtics-nets-playoffs.

Bates, Mike. "Yeah, the "Tomahawk Chop" bugs me. Here's why". *SBNation*, 1st May 2013. Accessed 28th August 2022. Available at: https://www.sbnation.com/mlb/2013/5/1/4292152/yeah-the-tomahawk-chop-bugs-me-heres-why.

Baxter, Kevin. "Mexicans call for answers after gruesome riot during Atlas vs. Querétaro soccer match". *Los Angeles Times*, 6th March 2022. Accessed 11th September 2022. Available at: https://www.latimes.com/sports/soccer/story/2022-03-06/commentary-mexicans-call-for-answers-after-gruesome-soccer-brawl.

BBC News. "Steward hurt in cricket chaos". *BBC News*, 17th June 2001. Accessed 28th August 2022. Available at: news.bbc.co.uk/2/hi/uk_news/1393761.stm.

BBC News. "Oxford Utd Swindon Town match: 13 fans arrested". *BBC News*, 4th March 2012. Accessed 28th August 2022. Available at: https://www.bbc.com/news/uk-england-oxfordshire-17249845.

BBC News. "Footballers Goodwillie and Robertson ruled as rapists". *BBC News*, 17th January 2017a. Accessed 12th September 2022. Available at: https://www.bbc.com/news/uk-scotland-edinburgh-east-fife-38651041.

BBC News. "Roman Zozulya: Player's Rayo Vallecano loan spell ends as fans call him Nazi". *BBC News*, 1st February 2017b. Accessed 12th December 2022. Available at: https://www.bbc.com/sport/football/38834539

BBC News. "Jamal Khashoggi: All you need to know about Saudi journalist's death". *BBC News*, 24th February 2021. Accessed 30th September 2022. Available at: https://www.bbc.com/news/world-europe-45812399

BBC Sport. "Euro 2022: England win over Germany watched by record television audience of 17.4m". *BBC Sport*, 1st August 2022. Accessed 18th

September 2022. Available at: https://www.bbc.com/sport/football /62375750#:~:text=Last%20year's%20Euro%202020%20final,Prince ss%20of%20Wales%20in%201997.

Beardsworth, James. "Soft power". *The Blizzard* 43 (2021): 37–44.

Behrens, Anton and Sebastian Uhrich. "Uniting a sport team's global fan community: Prototypical behavior of satellite fans enhances local fans' attitudes and perceptions of groupness". *European Sport Management Quarterly* 20(5) (2020): 598–617.

Belson, Ken. "Chris Borland Blasts N.F.L. for Hiding C.T.E. Risks". *The New York Times*, 24th October 2017. Accessed 18th September 2022. Available at: https://www.nytimes.com/2017/10/24/sports/football/chris -borland-nfl-cte.html.

Ben-Porat, Amir. "Football fandom: A bounded identification". *Soccer & Society* 11(3) (2010): 277–290.

Best, David. "The aesthetic in sport". *British Journal of Aesthetics* 14(3) (1974): 197–213.

Bonesteel, Matt and Marissa Payne. "Following anti-Semitic fan incident, Italian soccer orders part of Anne Frank's diary be read before games". *The Washington Post*, 24th October 2017. Accessed 28th August 2022. Available at: https://www.washingtonpost.com/news/early-lead/wp /2017/10/24/lazio-fans-leave-behind-anne-frank-stickers-in-latest -anti-semitic-gesture/.

Borge, Steffen. *The Philosophy of Football*. London: Routledge, 2019.

Brady, Michael. "Suffering in sport: Why people willingly embrace negative emotional experiences". *Journal of Philosophy of Sport* 46(2) (2019): 115–128.

Branscombe, Nyla R. and Daniel L. Wann. "The positive social and self-concept consequences of sports team identification". *Journal of Sport and Social Issues* 15(2) (1991): 115–127.

Caldwell, Dave. "Deshaun Watson's reputation is toxic. But do Browns fans care?". *The Guardian*, 23rd August 2022. Accessed 8th October 2022. Available at: https://www.theguardian.com/sport/2022/aug/23/ deshaun-watson-cleveland-browns-fans-nfl-football.

Campos, Sevanny. "Kansas City Chiefs fans donate over $300,000 to Buffalo children's hospital following playoff win over Bills". *CNBC*, 27th January 2022. Accessed 11th September 2022. Available at: https://www .cnbc.com/2022/01/27/kansas-city-chiefs-fans-donate-to-buffalo -childrens-hospital-after-win-over-bills.html.

Canada, Tracie and Chelsey R Carter. "The NFL's Racist 'Race Norming' Is an Afterlife of Slavery". *Scientific American*, 8th July 2021. Accessed 12th October 2022. Available at: https://www.scientificamerican.com/article/the-nfls-racist-race-norming-is-an-afterlife-of-slavery

Cardenas, Felipe. "Atlas FC-Querétaro match suspended due to fan violence; Liga MX calls off Sunday games". *The Athletic*, 6th March 2022. Accessed 11th September 2022. Available at: https://theathletic.com/news/atlas-fc-queretaro-match-suspended-due-to-fan-violence-liga-mx-calls-off-sunday-games/PVg7ltVZWpvj/.

Carlisle, Jeff. "USWNT, USMNT CBAs include equal pay: Why U.S. Soccer's new deals rewrite the history books". *ESPN*, 18th May 2022. Accessed 18th September 2022. Available at: https://www.espn.com/soccer/united-states-usa/story/4668917/uswntusmnt-cbas-include-equal-pay-why-us-soccers-new-deals-rewrite-the-history-books.

Cerami, Michael. "Somebody seriously just bought Ty Cobb's dentures at auction". *Bleacher Nation*, 12th September 2022. Accessed 22nd November 2022. Available at: https://www.bleachernation.com/baseballisfun/2022/09/12/how-much-would-you-pay-for-ty-cobbs-dentures-at-auction/.

Chiari, Mike. "Ravens OL John Urschel Retires After CTE Study, Continues Pursuit of MIT Ph.D.". *Bleacher Report*, 27th July 2017. Accessed 18th September 2022. Available at: https://bleacherreport.com/articles/2724133-ravens-ol-john-urschel-retires-after-cte-study-will-pursue-mit-doctorate.

Chirinos, Ella Adriana. "National identity and sports in Latin America: The hundred-hour football war between El Salvador and Honduras". *Mapping Politics* 9 (2018): 19–27.

Christopher, Paul. "Letter: "Bills Mafia" offends this Italian-American". *The Buffalo News*, 24th October 2020. Accessed 28th August 2022. Available at: https://buffalonews.com/opinion/letters/letter-bills-mafia-offends-this-italian-american/article_abc4783c-13c6-11eb-88b1-af40775ff391.html.

Cialdini, Robert B., Richard J. Borden, Avril Thorne, Marcus Randall Walker, Stephen Freeman and Lloyd Reynolds Sloan. "Basking in reflected glory: Three (football) field studies". *Journal of Personality and Social Psychology* 34(3) (1976): 366–375.

Cocking, Daniel and Jean Kennett. "Friendship and the self". *Ethics*, 108(3) (1998): 502–527.

Cocking, Dean and Jeanette Kennett "Friendship and moral danger". *Journal of Philosophy* 97(5) (2000): 278–296.

Cohan, Noah. *We Average Unbeautiful Watchers: Fan Narratives and the Reading of American Sports*. Lincoln: University of Nebraska Press, 2019.

Conn, David. "Manchester United fans prepare to show their true colours at Wembley". *The Guardian*, 27th February 2010. Accessed 18th September 2022. Available at: https://www.theguardian.com/sport/david-conn -inside-sport-blog/2010/feb/27/manchester-united-glazers-wembley -protest.

Corrigan, Dermot. "The case of Santi Mina: Guilty of sexual assault yet still playing football". *The Athletic*, 27th August 2022. Accessed 27th August 2022. Available at: https://theathletic.com/3538157/2022 /08/27/santi-mina-celta-saudi-arabia/?source=user-shared-article& redirected=1.

Crawford, Garry. *Consuming Sport: Fans, Sport and Culture*. London: Routledge, 2004.

Crook, David. "21 Years ago manchester city were relegated to the third tier". *Fansided*, 2019. Accessed 11th September 2022. Available at: https://mancitysquare.com/2019/05/03/21-years-ago-manchester -city-relegated-third-tier/.

Cross, John. "Arsene Wenger stunned by level of abuse from Arsenal supporters as Emirates mood turns nasty". *The Mirror*, 20th April 2016. Accessed 11th September 2022. Available at: https://www.mirror.co.uk /sport/football/news/arsene-wenger-stunned-level-abuse-7782518.

Cummings, Jim. "Why sports are a sad and dangerous waste of time". *Medium*, 30th August 2013. Accessed 10th October 2022. Available at: https://jimmycthatsme.medium.com/why-sports-are-a-sad-and -dangerous-waste-of-time-3530f0ee579a.

Davis, Paul. "The ladies of Beşiktaş: An example of moral and ideological ambiguity?". *Sport, Ethics and Philosophy* 6(1) (2012): 4–15.

Davis, Paul. "Football is football and is interesting, very interesting". *Sport, Ethics and Philosophy* 9(2) (2015): 140–152.

Davis, Paul. "The purist/partisan spectator discourse: Some examination and discrimination". *Sport, Ethics and Philosophy* 13(2) (2018): 247–258.

Devine, John William and Francisco Javier Lopez Frias. "Philosophy of sport". *The Stanford Encyclopedia of Philosophy* (Fall 2020 Edition), Edward N. Zalta (ed.). Available at: https://plato.stanford.edu/archives/fall2020/ entries/sport/.

Dixon, Nicholas. "The ethics of supporting sports teams". *Journal of Applied Philosophy* 18(2) (2001): 149–158.

Dixon, Nicholas. "In praise of partisanship". *Journal of the Philosophy of Sport* 43(2) (2016): 233–249.

Doyle, Jason P., Kevin Filo, Daniel Lock, Daniel C. Funk and Heath McDonald. "Exploring PERMA in spectator sport: Applying positive psychology to examine the individual-level benefits of sport consumption". *Sport Management Review* 19(5) (2016): 506–519.

Dyreson, Mark. "Globalizing the nation-making process: Modern sport in world history". *The International Journal of the History of Sport* 20(1) (2003): 91–106.

Edgar, Andrew. *Sport and Art: An Essay in the Hermeneutics of Sport*. London: Routledge, 2013.

Edgar, Andrew. "Three ways of watching a sports video". *Sport, Ethics and Philosophy* 10(4) (2016): 403–415.

Edgar, Andrew. "Super Leagues and Sacred Sites". *Sport, Ethics and Philosophy* 15(3) (2021): 205–207.

Edmundson, Mark. *Why Football Matters: My Education in the Game*. New York: Penguin Books, 2015.

Elias, Norbert and Eric Dunning. *Quest for Excitement. Sport and Leisure in the Civilizing Process*. Oxford: Basil Blackwell, 1986.

Elliott, Raymond Kenneth. "Aesthetics and sport". In Harold Whiting and D. Masterson (eds.) *Readings in the Aesthetics of Sport*. London: Lepus, 1974: 107–116.

Eror, Aleks. "The president ultra". *The Blizzard* 41 (2021): 17–30.

Erwin, Robert E. "Loyalty and virtues". *The Philosophical Quarterly* 42(169) (1992): 403–419.

eToro. "Cost of fandom in the premier league: The eToro fan financial statement". *Football Benchmark*, 12th November 2019. Accessed 30th August 2022. Available at: https://www.footballbenchmark.com/library/cost_of_fandom_in_the_premier_league_the_etoro_fan_financial_statement.

Fazal-E-Hasan, Syed Muhammad, Larry Neale, Harjit Sekhon, Gary Mortimer, Ian Brittain and Jaswinder Sekhon. "The path to game-day attendance runs through sports fan rituals". *Journal of Business Research* 137 (2021): 308–318.

Feezell, Randolph. *Sport, philosophy, and good lives*. Lincoln: University of Nebraska Press, 2013.

Fequiere, Pedro. "15 Really Unique Ways People Met Their Significant Others". *BuzzFeed*, 29th October. Accessed 11th September 2022. Available at: https://www.buzzfeed.com/pedrofequiere/15-really-strange-but -beautiful-ways-people-met-the-love-of.

Football Supporters' Association. *Women at the Match*. (2021) Available at: https://thefsa.org.uk/news/women-at-the-match-report-released/.

Foster, John. "Tell me how you play and i'll tell you who you are". In Ted Richards (ed.) *Soccer and Philosophy: Beautiful Thoughts on the Beautiful Game*. Open Court: Chicago, 2010, 253–264.

Foster Wallace, David. "Roger Federer as Religious Experience". *The New York Times*, 20th August 2006. Accessed 20th August 2022. Available online at: https://www.nytimes.com/2006/08/20/sports/playmagazine /20federer.html.

Fowles, Stacey May. *Baseball Life Advice: Loving the Game That Saved Me*. Toronto: McClelland & Stewart, 2017.

Fox, Dave. "The football match which started a war". *The False 9*, 25th April 2016. Accessed 11th September 2022. Available at: https://thefalse9 .com/2016/04/dinamo-red-star-boban-riot.html.

Fox, Kara. "Ponytails and smiles: Pervasive language keeps sexism in Olympic sport at play". CNN, 7th August 2021. Accessed 12th October 2022. Available online at: https://edition.cnn.com/2021/08/06/sport /olympics-sexism-women-sport-cmd-spt-intl/index.html

Fruh, Kyle, Alfred Archer and Jake Wojtowicz. "Sportswashing: Complicity and corruption". *Sport, Ethics and Philosophy* 17(1) (2023): 101–118.

Fruh, Kyle, Marcus Hedahl, Luke Maring and Nate Olson. "A fair shake for the fair-weather fan". *Journal of the Philosophy of Sport* 48(2) (2021): 262–274.

Galgano, Michael A, Robert Cantu and Lawrence S Chin. "Traumatic encephalopathy: The impact on athletes". *Cureus* 8(3) (2016): e532.

Gendreau, Megs S. "Why we care about who athletes are: on the peculiar nature of athletic achievement". *Journal of the Philosophy of Sport*, 49(2) (2022): 378–291.

Giulianotti, Richard. 'Supporters, followers, fans, and flâneurs: A taxonomy of spectator identities in football". *Journal of Sport and Social Issues* 26(1) (2002): 25–46.

Giulianotti, Richard. *Sport: A Critical Sociology*. Cambridge: Polity, 2016.

Gordon, James Bridget. "Throwback thursday: El Salvador vs Honduras (June 26th, 1969)". *Paste*, 14th July 2016. Accessed 11th September

2022. Available at https://www.pastemagazine.com/soccer/throwback -thursday-el-salvador-vs-honduras-june-26/

Gough, Christina. "Share of sports fans in the United States as of May 2022". *Statista.com*, 10th June 2022. Accessed 10th October 2022. Available at: https://www.statista.com/statistics/300148/interest-nfl-football-age -canada/.

Greene, David. "Sports teams consider changing team names amid racial reckoning". *NPR: Morning Edition*, 10th July 2020. Accessed 18th September 2022. Available at: https://www.npr.org/2020/07/10/889653163/ sports-teams-consider-changing-team-names-amid-racial-reckoning.

Gumbrecht, Hans Ulrich. *In Praise of Athletic Beauty*. Cambridge, MA: The Belknap Press of Harvard University Press, 2006.

Halliday, Josh. "Man United's Mason Greenwood further arrested on suspicion of sexual assault and threats to kill". *The Guardian*, 1st February 2022. Accessed 12th September 2022. Available at: https://www .theguardian.com/uk-news/2022/feb/01/man-utd-footballer-mason -greenwood-further-arrested-over-sexual-assault.

Harmsen, Natalie. "Toronto maple leafs tattoos are the most popular of any sports team in the world". *Complex Canada*, 12th May 2021. Accessed 30th August 2022. Available at: https://www.complex.com/sports/toronto -maple-leafs-tattoos-are-the-most-popular-of-any-sports-team.

Hedges, Matthew. "An Ally Held me as a spy: And the west is complicit". *The Atlantic*, 25th January 2019. Accessed 5th October 2022. Available at: https://www.theatlantic.com/international/archive/2019/01/ matthew-hedges-uae-held-me-spy-west-complicit/581200/.

Hewitt, Reed. "Deshaun Watson's allegations raise questions for female Cleveland browns fans". *The Lion*, July 12th 2022. Accessed 8th October 2022. Available at: thelion.sites.lmu.edu/sports/deshaun-watsons-alleg ations-raises-questions-for-female-cleveland-browns-fans/.

Hirst, Paul. "Tottenham v West Ham: Hammers fans issued with warning over anti-Semitic chanting". *The Independent*, 4th October 2013. Accessed 28th August 2022. Available at: https://www.independent.co.uk/sport/ football/premier-league/tottenham-v-west-ham-hammers-fans-issued -with-warning-over-antisemitic-chanting-8858879.html.

Hobsbawm, Eric. *Nations and Nationalism since 1780: Programme, Myth, Reality.* Cambridge: Cambridge University Press, 1990.

Hornby, Nick, *Fever Pitch*. London: Gollancz, 1992.

Howard, George Elliott. "Social psychology of the spectator". *American Journal of Sociology* 18(1) (1912): 33–50.

Howe, Leslie A. "Bad faith, bad behaviour, and role models". *Journal of Applied Philosophy* 37(5) (2020): 764–780.

Huizinga, Johan. *Homo Ludens: A Study of the Play-element in Culture*. London: Routledge, 2014.

Inglehart, Ronald F. *Religion's Sudden Decline: What's Causing it, and What Comes Next?* New York: Oxford University Press, 2021.

Jollimore, Troy. *Love's Vision*. Princeton: Princeton University Press, 2011.

Jolly, Richard. "Support that never wavered for Man City". *The National*, 26th September 2011. Accessed 11th September 2022. Available at: https://www.thenationalnews.com/sport/support-that-never-wavered -for-man-city-1.356307#:~:text=City's%20average%20attendance% 20in%20the,clubs%20all%20over%20the%20division.

Jones, Tobias. "At home with Italy's ultras: 'It isn't about watching football, but watching each other'". *The Guardian*, 15th September 2019. Accessed 28th August 2022. Available at: https://www.theguardian.com/books /2019/sep/15/at-home-with-the-italian-ultras-football-fans-cosenza -tobias-jones.

Jones, Tobias. "Inside Italy's ultras: The dangerous fans who control the game". *The Guardian*, 1st December 2016. Accessed 28th August 2022. Available at: https://www.theguardian.com/world/2016/ dec/01/nside-talys-ultras-the-dangerous-fans-who-control-the- game.

Jones, Tobias. *Ultra: The Underworld of Italian Football*. London: Head of Zeus, 2019.

Kadlac, Adam. *The Ethics of Sports Fandom*. New York: Routledge, 2022.

Kalman-Lamb, Nathan, "Imagined communities of fandom: Sport, spectatorship, meaning and alienation in late capitalism". *Sport in Society* 24(6) (2021): 922–936.

Kapuściński, Ryszard. "The soccer war". *Harper's Magazine* 272 (June 1986): 47–55. Accessed 5th October 2022. Available at: https://harpers.org /2015/06/the-soccer-war/.

Keegan, Mike. "Blackburn fans launch crowdfunding page to raise £20,000 for dementia-suffering club hero Tony Parkes as the PFA is unwilling to contribute to the former midfielder's care fees". *Mail Online*, 1st February 2022. Accessed 11th September 2022. Available at: https://www

.dailymail.co.uk/sport/football/article-10465931/Blackburn-Rovers
-fans-launch-fundraiser-dementia-suffering-Tony-Parkes-PFA-refused
-help.html.

Kleinig, John. "Loyalty". In Edward N. Zalta (ed.) *The Stanford Encyclopedia of Philosophy* (Summer 2022 Edition). Available at: https://plato.stanford
.edu/archives/sum2022/entries/loyalty/

Koebert, Josh. "The NFL fans who spend the most and least money on their team [2021 survey]". *Finance Buzz*, 9th August 2021. Accessed 30th August 2022. Available at: https://financebuzz.com/nfl-fan-spending.

Kolodny, Niko. "Love as valuing a relationship". *The Philosophical Review* 112(2) (2003): 135–189.

Lanchester, John, "Getting into esports". *London Review of Books* 42(16) (2020). Available at: https://ewww.lrb.co.uk/the-paper/v42/n16/
john-lanchester/diary

Lasch, Christopher. *The Culture of Narcissism: American Life in an Age of Diminishing Expectations*. New York: WW Norton & Company, 1979.

Litman, Laken. "Alabama fan attended 781 consecutive games before passing away". *For The Win*, 24th June 2013. Accessed 30th August 2022. Available online at: https://ftw.usatoday.com/2013/06/alabama-fan
-attended-781-consecutive-games-before-passing-away.

López Frías, Francisco Javier. "The psycho: Biological bases of sports supporters' behaviour: The virtuous supporter". *Sport, Ethics and Philosophy* 6(4) (2012): 423–438.

Lopez-Cantero, Pilar and Alfred Archer. "Lost without you: The Value of Falling out of Love". *Ethical Theory and Moral Practice* 23(3–4) (2020): 515–529.

Lowe, Sid. *Fear and Loathing in La Liga*. London: Yellow Jersey Press, 2013.

MacInnes, Paul. "England fan disorder at Euro 2020 final almost led to deaths, review finds". *The Guardian*, 3rd December 2021. Accessed 28th August 2022. Available at: http://www.theguardian.com/football
/2021/dec/03/england-fan-disorder-at-euro-2020-final-almost-led
-to-deaths-review-finds.

Magee, Aidan. "Is this football's greatest superfan? 1,503 matches in a row and still counting...". *Sky Sports News*, 14th May 2020. Accessed 30th August 2022. Available at: https://www.skysports.com/football/news
/11711/11988102/is-this-footballs-greatest-superfan-1-503-matches
-in-a-row-and-still-counting.

Maske, Mark. "Not ready for prime time". *TheWashington Post*, 17th September 2002. Available at: https://www.washingtonpost.com/wp-dyn/articles /A26242-2002Sep16.html.

Matthew, Shaj. "Why did Borges hate soccer?". *The New Republic*, 10th October 2014. Accessed 10th October 2022. Available at: https:// newrepublic.com/article/118228/world-cup-2014-why-did -borges-hate-soccer.

Milekić, Svan. "1990 Football riot becomes national myth in Croatia". *Balkan Transitional Justice*, 13th May 2016. Accessed 11th September 2022. Available at: https://balkaninsight.com/2016/05/13/1990-football -riot-remains-croatia-s-national-myth-05-12-2016/.

Morgan, Emmanuel and Remy Tumin. "For Browns, Deshaun Watson is a $230 million question mark". *The NewYork Times*, 9th June 2022. Accessed 8th October 2022. Available at: https://www.nytimes.com/2022/06 /09/sports/football/deshaun-watson-browns.html.

Morris, Charlie. *Generation Game: One Football Club, One Family and a Century of Obsession*. Croydon: Goldford, 2019.

Mumford, Stephen. "Allegiance and identity". *Journal of the Philosophy of Sport* 31(2) (2004): 184–195.

Mumford, Stephen. *Watching Sport: Aesthetics, Ethics and Emotion*. London: Routledge, 2012a.

Mumford, Stephen. "Moderate partisanship as oscillation". *Sport, Ethics and Philosophy* 6(3) (2012b): 369–375.

Mumford, Stephen. *A Philosopher Looks at Sport*. Cambridge: Cambridge University Press, 2021.

Newson, Martha, Michael Buhrmester and Harvey Whitehouse. "United in defeat: Shared suffering and group bonding among football fans". *Managing Sport and Leisure* (2021): 1–18. Online First.

Nguyen, C. Thi. *Games: Agency as Art*. New York: Oxford University Press, 2020.

Nozick, Robert. *Examined Life: Philosophical Meditations*. New York: Simon and Schuster, 1989.

NPR. "What it means for sports fans' mental health when their team loses". NPR, 14th February 2022. Accessed 30th August 2022. Available at: https://www.npr.org/2022/02/14/1080684282/what-it-means-for -sports-fans-mental-health-when-their-team-loses

Nussbaum, Martha C. *Political Emotions:Why Love Matters for Justice*. Cambridge, MA: Harvard University Press, 2013.

Old Firm Facts. "Rangers reaction shows classism is alive and well when it comes to Scottish football". *Not the Old Firm*, 10th March 2021. Accessed 10th October 2022. Available at: https://www.nottheoldfirm.com/columnist/rangers-reaction-shows-classism-is-alive-and-well-when-it-comes-to-scottish-football/.

Olmsted, Larry. *Fans: How Watching Sports Makes us Happier, Healthier, and More Understanding*. New York: Workman Publishing, 2021.

Oosterbaan, Martijn and Martine Prange. *Vrouwenvoetbal in Nederland: Spiegel en katalysator van maatschappelijke verandering*. Utrecht: Uitgeverij Klement, 2017.

Orwell, George. "The sporting spirit". In George Orwell (ed.) *Shooting an Elephant*. London: Penguin, 2003.

Pandian, Ananth. "LOOK: Fan gets buried in Redskins-themed coffin". *Commanders Wire*, 20th September 2018. Accessed 30th August 2022. Available at: https://commanderswire.usatoday.com/2018/09/30/look-fan-gets-buried-in-redskins-themed-coffin/.

Pantelick, Nicolas. "Fanaticism and the 'ultras' movement: How far will you go to support your team?". *Harvard International Review*, 2nd February 2022. Accessed 28th August 2022. Available at: https://hir.harvard.edu/fanaticism-and-the-ultras-movement/.

Partick Thistle. "Partick thistle family club". *PTFC.co.uk*, 19th May 2020a. Accessed 11th September 2022. Available at: https://ptfc.co.uk/ptfc-news/partick-thistle-family-club/.

Partick Thistle. "Partick Thistle Charitable Trust deliver 9,000 meals locally to help vulnerable communities during Covid-19 crisis". *PTFC.co.uk*, 18th May 2020b. Accessed 11th September 2022. Available at: https://ptfc.co.uk/ptfc-news/partick-thistle-charitable-trust-deliver-9000-meals-locally-to-help-vulnerable-communities-during-covid-19-crisis/.

Partick Thistle. "Glasgow patients boosted by £3275 Jags NHS strip donation". *PTFC.co.uk*, 1st October 2020c. Accessed 11th September 2022. Available at: https://ptfc.co.uk/ptfc-news/glasgow-patients-boosted-by-3275-jags-nhs-strip-donation/.

Phillips, Carron J. "Jimmy Haslam is to blame for the vile T-shirts and signs in support of Deshaun Watson". *Deadspin*, 23rd August 2022. Accessed 8th October 2022. Available at: https://deadspin.com/jimmy-haslam-is-to-blame-for-the-vile-t-shirts-and-sign-1849446316.

Pope, Stacey. "'The love of my life' The meaning and importance of sport for female fans". *Journal of Sport and Social Issues* 37(2) (2013): 176–195.

Protasi, Sara. "Loving people for who they are (even when they don't love you back)". *European Journal of Philosophy* 24(1) (2016): 214–234.

Quinn, Kevin G. *Sports and Their Fans: The History, Economics and Culture of the Relationship Between Spectator and Sport*. Jefferson: McFarland and Co., 2009.

Rey, Daniel. "Black and white wash". *The Blizzard* 43 (2021): 44–47.

Richards, Alex. "England fan with flare up bum 'strolled into Wembley without ticket' after 12-hour bender". *The Mirror*, 25th July 2021. Accessed 28th August 2022. Available at: https://www.mirror.co.uk/sport/football/news/england-football-yob-boasts-12-24538423.

Robshaw, Brandon. "In answer to Orwell: A defence of international sport". *Journal of the Philosophy of Sport* 48(1) (2021): 1–9.

Rosenwald, Michael S. "NFL's John Urschel has a brain made for math. And he's willing to risk it on the field". *The Washington Post*, 9th October 2016. Accessed 18th September 2022. Available at: https://www.washingtonpost.com/local/raven-john-urschels-brain-is-made-for-math-and-hes-willing-to-risk-it-on-the-field/2016/10/08/845a65ce-8c8c-11e6-bf8a-3d26847eeed4_story.html.

Ross, Peter. *The Passion of Harry Bingo*. Dingwall: Sandstone Press, 2017.

Royals.org. "Division table + stats (98–99)". *Royals.org*, 1999. Accessed 11th September 2022. Available at: https://www.royals.org/table99.html.

Rubin, John. *You Don't Know Who You Are*. Glasgow, Scotland: Partick Thistle Football Club, 2015. Accessed 13 Jan 2020. Available online at: http://www.jonrubin.net/you-dont-know-who-you-are.

Rudy, Kathy. *Loving Animals: Toward a New Animal Advocacy*. Minneapolis: University of Minnesota Press, 2011.

Rushden, Max. "How to tackle misogyny in football: Football weekly special". *Guardian Football Weekly Podcast*, 1st December 2021. Accessed 7th October 2022. Available at: https://www.theguardian.com/football/audio/2021/dec/01/how-to-tackle-misogyny-in-football-football-weekly-special.

Rushden, Max. "Shutdowns, FIFA and Dealing with a General Lack of Football". *Guardian Football Weekly*, 16th March 2020. Accessed 19 Feb 2021. Available at: https://www.theguardian.com/football/audio/2020/mar/16/shutdowns-fifa-and-dealing-with-a-general-lack-of-football-football-weekly-podcast.

Russell, John S. "The ideal fan or good fans?". *Sport, Ethics and Philosophy* 6(1) (2012): 16–30.

Russell, Shahan. "The real football war! When El Salvador invaded Honduras over a soccer game". *War History Online*, June 20th 2016. Accessed 11th September 2022. Available at: https://www.warhistoryonline.com/history/the-real-football-war.html.

Rutherford, Jeremy. "'It's truly an honor': Why fans name children after their Blues heroes and what the players say about it". *The Athletic*, 7th February 2020. Accessed 22nd November 2022. Available at: https://theathletic.com/1440115/2020/02/07/its-truly-an-honor-why-fans-name-their-children-after-their-blues-heroes-and-what-the-players-say-about-it/

Ryall, Emily. *Philosophy of Sport: Key Questions*. London: Bloomsbury Publishing, 2016.

Sandvoss, Cornel. *Fans: The Mirror of Consumption*. Cambridge: Polity, 2005.

Sano, Joelle and John B. Williamson. "Factors affecting union decline in 18 OECD countries and their implications for labor movement reform". *International Journal of Comparative Sociology* 49(6)6 (2008): 479–500.

Sherman, Nancy. "Aristotle on friendship and the shared life". *Philosophy and Phenomenological Research* 47(4) (1987): 589–613.

Shpall, Sam. "A tripartite theory of love". *Journal of Ethics and Social Philosophy* 13(20) (2018): 91–124.

Snyder, C. Richard, MaryAnne Lassegard and Carol E. Ford. "Distancing after group success and failure: Basking in reflected glory and cutting off reflected failure". *Journal of Personality and Social Psychology* 51(2) (1986): 382–388.

Spurgin, Earl. "Hey, How did I become a Role Model? Privacy and the Extent of Role-Model Obligations". *Journal of Applied Philosophy* 29(2) (2012): 118–132.

Staufenberg, Jess. "Chelsea football fan and top corporate lawyer sacked for "Scouse scum" rant". *The Independent*, 9th September 2015. Accessed 28th August 2022. Available at: https://www.independent.co.uk/news/uk/home-news/chelsea-football-fan-and-top-corporate-lawyer-sacked-for-scouse-scum-rant-a6727126.html.

Stear, Nils-Hennes. "Sport, Make-Believe, and Volatile Attitudes". *The Journal of Aesthetics and Art Criticism* 75(3) (2017): 275–288.

Suits, Bernard. *The Grasshopper: Games, Life and Utopia*. Peterborough, ON: Broadview Press, 2014.

Tännsjö, Torbjörn. "Is our admiration for sports heroes fascistoid?". *Journal of the Philosophy of Sport* 25(1) (1998): 23–34.

Why It's OK to Be a Sports Fan

Tarver, Erin C. *The I in Team: Sports Fandom and the Reproduction of Identity*. Chicago: The University of Chicago Press, 2017.

Tate, Tim. *Secret History of Women's Football*. London: Kings Road Publishing, 2013.

Taylor, Richard. *Good and Evil*. London: Macmillan, 1970

Tomasetti, Kathryn. "Chanting alongside Istanbul's female football fans". *Rutherford & Tomasetti Travel Writers*, December 2015. Accessed 28th August 2022. Available at: https://www.rutherfordtomasetti.com/istanbul -turkey-female-football-fan.

Tyler, George. "The moral responsibility of fandom". *Journal of the Philosophy of Sport* 48(1) (2021): 111–128.

US Soccer. "U.S. Soccer Federation, Women's and Men's Nation Team Unions Agree to Historic Collective Bargaining Agreements". *US Soccer*, 18th May 2022. Accessed 18th September 2022. Available at: https://www .ussoccer.com/stories/2022/05/ussf-womens-and-mens-national -team-unions-agree-to-historic-collective-bargaining-agreements

Victory, Dennis. "Brawl erupts during Carver-Montgomery vs. Valley game; fight spills over into stands by Dennis Victory". *The Birmingham News*, 17th February 2009. Accessed 28th August 2022. Available at: https://web .archive.org/web/20160303191500/http://www.al.com/sports/ birmingham/index.ssf/2009/02/carvermontgomery_vs_valley_gam .html.

Walton, Kendall. "'It's only a game!': Sports as fiction". In Kendall Walton (ed.) *In Other Shoes: Music, Metaphor, Empathy, Existence*. Oxford: Oxford University Press, 2015: 75–83.

Wann, Daniel L. and Jeffrey D. James. *Sport Fans: The Psychology and Social Impact of Fandom*. New York: Routledge, 2018.

Wann, Daniel L. and Nancy H. Fast. "Using sport fandom to aid in the search for meaning". *Findings in Sport Hospitality Entertainment and Event Management* (2021).

Wann, Daniel L., Josh Polk and Gentzy Franz. "Examining the state social psychological health benefits of identifying with a distant sport team". *Journal of Sport Behavior* 34(2) (2011a): 188–205.

Wann, Daniel L., Kelly Rogers, Keith Dooley and Mary Foley. "Applying the team identification: Social psychological health model to older sport fans". *The International Journal of Aging and Human Development* 72(4) (2011b): 303–315.

Weaver, Levi. "On minor-league pay, MLB's stance doesn't line up with the facts". *The Athletic*, 4th April 2018. Accessed 18th September 2022. Available at: https://theathletic.com/293189/2018/04/04/on-minor-league-pay-mlbs-stance-doesnt-line-up-with-the-facts/?redirected=1

Wellman, Christopher. "Do celebrated athletes have special responsibilities to be good role models? An imagined dialog between Charles Barkley and Karl Malone". In Jan Boxill (ed.) *Sports Ethics: An Anthology*. Malden: Blackwell Publishing, 2003: 333–336.

Whitehead, Jacob. "New report demonstrates causal link between head impacts and CTE for first time". *The Athletic*, 26th July 2022. Accessed 30th September 2022. Available at: https://theathletic.com/3449702/2022/07/26/new-report-head-impact-cte/.

Whitehouse, Harvey, Jonathan Jong, Michael D. Buhrmester, Ángel Gómez, Brock Bastian, Christopher M. Kavanagh, Martha Newson et al. "The evolution of extreme cooperation via shared dysphoric experiences". *Scientific Reports* 7(1) (2017): 1–10.

Wilczek, Maria. "Rage against the regime: The Belarus ultras who stood up to Lukashenko". *The New Statesman*, 14th May 2022. Accessed 28th August 2022. Available at: https://www.newstatesman.com/world/europe/2022/05/rage-against-the-regime-the-belarus-ultras-who-stood-up-to-lukashenko.

Wildman, Nathan. "Don't stop make-believing". *Journal of the Philosophy of Sport* 46(2) (2019): 261–275.

Williams, Jean. *A Beautiful Game: International Perspectives on Women's Football*. Oxford: Berg, 2007.

Wilson, Brian. "The 'anti-jock' movement: Reconsidering youth resistance, masculinity, and sport culture in the age of the Internet". *Sociology of Sport Journal* 19(2) (2002): 206–233.

Wilson, Fraser. "Ian McCall on phoning Partick Thistle fans and life's 'bigger challenges' than football struggles". *Daily Record*, 21st March 2020. Accessed 11th September 2022. Available at: https://www.dailyrecord.co.uk/sport/football/football-news/ian-mccall-phoning-partick-thistle-21728361

Wilson, Jonathan. *Inverting the Pyramid: The History of Soccer Tactics (Fully Revised & Updated)*. New York: Orion, 2018.

Wilson, Jonathan. "The balance between admiring man city's play, condemning its alleged misdeeds". *Sports Illustrated*, 17th May 2019a.

Accessed 11th September 2022. Available at: https://www.si.com/soccer/2019/05/17/manchester-city-success-ownership-controversy-uefa-investigation

Wilson, Jonathan. *The Names Heard Long Ago: How the Golden Age of Hungarian Soccer Shaped the Modern Game*. New York: Bold Type Books, 2019b.

Wojtowicz, Jake. "Fans, identity, and punishment". *Sport, Ethics and Philosophy* 15(1) (2021): 59–73.

Wolf, Susan. "Happiness and meaning: Two aspects of the good life". *Social Philosophy and Policy* 14(1) (1997): 207–25.

Wolf, Susan. *Meaning in Life and Why It Matters*. Princeton: Princeton University Press, 2010.

Wuertz, Sadie. "More than the uniform: Volleyball players speak out about body image and sexism". *The Beacon*, 6th November 2021. Accessed 12th October 2022. Available at: https://www.upbeacon.com/article/2021/11/more-than-the-uniform-volleyball-players-speak-out-about-body-image-and-sexism.

Yorke, Christopher C. and Alfred Archer. "Ambassadors of the game: do famous athletes have special obligations to act virtuously?". *Journal of the Philosophy of Sport* 47(2) (2020): 301–317.

Why It's OK to Be a Sports Fan

Printed in the United States
by Baker & Taylor Publisher Services